Praise for

Browsing Nature's Aisles

Browsing Nature's Aisles is an inspiring journal of
one family's effort to break free from manufactured foods,
and transition to home-grown and locally-sourced cuisine,
supplemented by a steady diet of wild fare. It is a great read
for those who dream of getting back to the land and
becoming more self-sufficient, yet don't know where to start.
Come along for the journey as authors Wendy and Eric
Brown overcome the learning curve to successfully blend
wild plants, fungi, and game into their regular diet.

—THOMAS J. ELPEL, author, *Botany in a Day:*
The Patterns Method of Plant Identification

The Browns are the inspiring Pied Pipers of
suburban homesteaders. Through their finely tuned,
personal account of the untapped and tasty world of wild
foraging, you'll be craving those dandelion greens
right out your doorstep.

—LISA KIVIRIST & JOHN IVANKO, coauthors,
Farmstead Chef & *Rural Renaissance*

As a species we have developed over millions of years
an acute ability to forage for our foods in nature. *Browsing
Natures Aisles* is a shining example of reestablishing that
connection between nature and our foods. For anyone with
an interest in food security, foraging or shifting the way
they think about food, this is a must read.

—DAN AGRO, owner, AgroMyco

As engrossing as a seed catalog and much more truthful, this tells a great story about the adventures, delights and disappointments of foraging for all manners of wild foods. A new generation of homesteaders, nature enthusiasts, hikers, campers and would-be foragers have long awaited these passionate, compelling and hard-earned words of wisdom. This enormously useful, inspirational volume is a significant and original contribution.

—Connie Krochmal, garden writer and columnist, *Bee Culture* magazine

BROWSING
NATURE'S
AISLES

BROWSING NATURE'S AISLES

A YEAR of
FORAGING for WILD FOOD
in the SUBURBS

Wendy & Eric Brown

new society
PUBLISHERS

Paperback ISBN: 978-0-86571-750-3 eISBN: 978-1-55092-540-1

Inquiries regarding requests to reprint all or part of *Browsing Nature's Aisles*
should be addressed to New Society Publishers at the address below.

To order directly from the publishers, please call toll-free
(North America) 1-800-567-6772, or order online at www.newsociety.com

Any other inquiries can be directed by mail to:

New Society Publishers
P.O. Box 189, Gabriola Island, BC V0R 1X0, Canada
(250) 247-9737

New Society Publishers' mission is to publish books that contribute in fundamental ways to
building an ecologically sustainable and just society, and to do so with the least possible impact on the environment, in a manner that models this vision. We are committed to doing
this not just through education, but through action. The interior pages of our bound books
are printed on Forest Stewardship Council®-registered acid-free paper that is **100% post-
consumer recycled** (100% old growth forest-free), processed chlorine free, and printed
with vegetable-based, low-VOC inks, with covers produced using FSC®-registered stock.
New Society also works to reduce its carbon footprint, and purchases carbon offsets based on
an annual audit to ensure a carbon neutral footprint. For further information, or to browse
our full list of books and purchase securely, visit our website at: **www.newsociety.com**

LIBRARY AND ARCHIVES CANADA CATALOGUING IN PUBLICATION

Brown, Wendy, 1967-, author
Browsing nature's aisles : a year of foraging for wild food in the suburbs / Wendy &
Eric Brown.

Includes bibliographical references and index.
ISBN 978-0-86571-750-3 (pbk.)

1. Wild plants, Edible--Identification. 2. Cooking (Wild foods).
3. Food--Preservation. 4. Food--Safety measures. 5. Sustainable living.

I. Brown, Eric, 1969-, author II. Title.

TX823.B76 2013   641.6   C2013-904396-9

To Kaya, Etain and Tehya
who are always great sports and
amazing young women

Contents

Acknowledgments

ONE OF THE BEST PARTS OF WRITING A BOOK (other than the amazing adventure it is, in general) is the opportunity to express our gratitude, in writing, to the people who helped to make it happen. We are blessed to have a wonderful community of people who helped us in some way to make this particular book happen, because, really, when we started this project, it wasn't just the two of us, in isolation, wandering around and munching wild plants. From the beginning, we knew we would be roping a lot of other people into our crazy scheme.

On that note, we owe a huge thanks to our three daughters, Kaya, Etain and Tehya, who tagged along on this incredible journey and never failed to remind us to play as much as we worked. They were the reason we wanted to try this different way of nourishing our bodies, but we were also asking them to make some significant changes in their diets — which was a pretty big deal for at least one of the three, who has very specific likes and dislikes when it comes to what she eats. We are incredibly grateful for the willingness of all three to indulge us.

We are also very grateful to our community of friends and family who not only braved the possibility of being fed foods that we foraged, but some of whom rose to the occasion and foraged some of their own to share with us. We are humbled by their adventurous spirits and support, and while the list is long, we felt it important to try to acknowledge each of them: Whitney, Trinity and Dakota Antoine; Crystal, Amber, and Lauren Arsenault; Amanda Bell; Ruby Bertrand; Richard, Melissa, West, and Tega Bourgeois-Lang; Ben Brookes; Dustin Brown; Emma Brown; Lisa and Sarah Card; Carol and Ron Doucette; Gar (a.k.a. Patricia Redlon); Liz Glidden; Joe Gresik; Andy, Margaret, and Lila Happel; Shawn, Lori, Tori, and Isaac Hussey; Tina and Ashley Jolly; Vicky Lloyd; Charlene Lopresti; Chad and Candi Maloney; Jake Maloney; Josh Maloney; Chris Mansfield; Richard, Lynn, Bre, Megan, and Michael Neal; Mariel Roy; Tad, Darnell and Marissa Stuart; and Charlie, Linda and Amelia Whitten. We are truly blessed to know all of these wonderful people.

We are especially thankful for our dear friend, Crystal Arsenault from Capture the Moment Photography for her unflappable nature and willingness to travel anywhere we've asked, at any time of the year to catch the perfect shot; and our most ardent supporter (and Number One fan), Melissa Bourgeois-Lang, who is ever enthusiastic in helping to spread the word and is incredibly expressive in her fervor for what we do.

There are several people who have served in the role of teacher, and without them, none of this would have been possible, because we would not know what we know without their guidance. Through her own writing, Aunt Connie (Krochmal) inspired us to begin this project, and she continues to encourage us to keep learning and growing. Our mentors, Chris and Ashirah Knapp, Mike Dimauro, Dan Agro, and Lesley and Freda Paul took the time to patiently guide us in the ways of respectful, grateful gathering of the wild foods that surround us. Authors and role models, Thomas Elpel, Sam Thayer, and Stephen Buhner, helped us to see that Mother Nature offers so much, if only we take the time to look, and that it is possible to find food everywhere.

A final thanks is offered to our New Society Publishers family for their kind support and fierce determination to make this a better world. In particular, we are grateful to: Ingrid Witvoet, who saw fit to allow us to share our thoughts and experiences once again; Sue Custance, who has sent firm, but gentle, reminders from the beginning to the end to make sure the book stayed on track; Judith Brand, whose enthusiasm and dedication made this book what it is, as opposed to what we managed to cobble together; and EJ Hurst and Sara Reeves, who have worked really hard to get this book out into the world for all to see.

We are incredibly blessed to be supported, and loved, by so many people. Our gratitude is heartfelt and often overwhelming. To all of those listed above and those who share our circle, we humbly offer a simple "thank you."

Preface

IT WAS QUIET BACK IN THE WOODS, although we could hear the whine of the occasional car passing out on the road. Many of the trees had lost their foliage in preparation for a winter's sleep, but the mix of conifers and deciduous trees muffled all of the noises of modern life except the crunching of our feet as we shuffled through the dead leaves on the forest floor.

Ordinarily, I am a stick-to-the-path kind of person. I enjoy walks through the woods, but I prefer to stay out of the underbrush and stick to the obviously well-traveled walkways. Today was no leisurely stroll. We were on a mission.

Eric was looking up into the skeletal branches, paying particular attention to the white-barked birch trees that stood out brightly in the dark forest. We were in search of the elusive chaga (*Inonotus obliquus*), often referred to as a "mushroom" and certainly one of the many tree spore parasites, but very uncharacteristic in its growth habits as compared to other true mushrooms. Chaga is renowned for its healing properties. We wanted some.

I did not really know what to look for. Every dark spot on the white-barked birch looked like chaga ... and nothing did. I shuffled through the dead leaves, trying to keep up, but mostly not being successful. In an effort to keep my footing, I looked down at the forest floor. A thick growth of a dark green-leafed plant caught my attention. It was everywhere, and so dark green that it contrasted sharply with brown decay. I'd never noticed anything like it before, and I had no idea what it was.

"What do you think that is?" I called to Eric, who was walking around a large birch a few yards from where I was standing in a patch of the green stuff.

"I don't know," he replied.

"Some sort of winter green, for sure," I said to him.

Eric and I have been studying plant identification for years, mostly as hobbyists, and we have close to a dozen books on various wild edible and medicinal plants. We had a long list of ones that we could identify as being safe to eat, but a considerably shorter list of those that we could identify and knew how to prepare as food. For years, we dabbled here and there at finding things to eat out in the forest or other wild places we occasion, but we had yet to make foraging a regular part of what we do.

There are some wild foods that we enjoy every year. Maple sap is one of the foraged foods that we have enjoyed for several years. Although some people may argue that sugaring is not wild harvesting (and certainly not in the Sam Thayer sautéed-spring-greens-with-wild-leeks kind of way), the fact is that we do not have a cultivated maple forest.

We have also harvested other wild foods. One summer a friend dragged us off to a clear-cut area where we picked blueberries as big as chickpeas. Later that year, we hit the mother lode of wild blackberries (*Rubus fruticosus*) just off a favorite walking path and filled several buckets. Occasionally, we collected a meal's worth of stinging nettles or dandelion (*Taraxacum officinale*) greens. However, like most people, with the exception of our annual maple syrup harvest, wild edibles were not a regular part of our diet.

The reason is simple. Like most people, we did not know enough about cooking with wild plants. There are hundreds of cookbooks on the market that use, what we believe, are exotic ingredients, like eggplant, but try finding a non-foraging-specific cookbook that has recipes for common plantain (*Plantago major*), or nettles or acorns, and be prepared to be disappointed. Further, wild foraging books are so full of complicated descriptions of ways to prepare the food to make it safe that it is daunting, to say the least.

It has only been a few years since we transitioned from the typical American processed foods diet to a local foods diet. Initially, it was a struggle learning how to cook the foods from the local farmer's market (before we started growing them, in quantity, in our home garden). When one is accustomed to cooking packaged food where the most complicated instruction is "add water," and then one must learn to cook less familiar vegetables like rutabaga and Hubbard squash, there can be a pretty steep learning curve. Take that to the next level of needing to learn not just how to cook the very different foods, but first how to correctly identify them, and it is easy to understand why the average person usually does not bother, and why it took us so long to take that step from knowing about all of the wild foods to really getting to know them. At least at the farmer's market what we bought could be presumed safe to eat without complicated conjuring and magic spells, which always seemed to be part of the process with wild foods.

For a very long time, wild edibles remained a curiosity, but not a dietary staple.

Over the last few years, however, almost daily we would see a news story on the dangers of eating just about anything from the grocery store shelves. A recent article warned against eating corn-based products, as most of the corn served in this country is from genetically engineered (GE) seed, which recent studies suggest are linked to long-term health problems. A grocery shopping guide in PDF form accompanied the article. So, I opened the PDF file and was looking through the products that were okay to eat and the companies who pledged to use no GE ingredients or genetically modified organisms (GMO).

Since we embarked on a local foods diet, what not to eat has been a frequent topic of conversation in our house. Between not allowing ourselves to eat foods that are not grown in our local area and trying to avoid those that might contain questionably safe ingredients, the list of what is off-limits seems to grow every day. We now purchase nothing containing high-fructose corn syrup, stay away from anything with a benzoate in it, avoid meat from a factory farm, never use foods preserved in BPA-lined cans (which is all of them) and eschew any fruits or vegetables not grown in Maine. I never thought enough about what effect these conversations might be having on my daughters until that day when I opened that PDF and was skimming through the list.

My daughters were in the room with me, and I looked over to see my nine-year-old crying. I asked her what was wrong, and she said, "I'm afraid I'm going to eat something that will hurt me."

And there I was, between that proverbial rock and hard place. I could ignore what I knew and feed my children those foods. I could stop talking to them about why I make the food choices I make, but then I might get caught in a "because I said so" argument when they want the food that I cannot, in good conscience, allow them to eat, and I have to give them a reason why that food is not okay. They are not stupid, and they deserve the truth, but it is tough when the truth is scary enough to bring them to tears.

At that point, I knew we needed to make the shift from literally handing our lives over to the industrial food complex and hoping they will not poison us, too quickly, to being empowered to find our own food — for my daughters' sake. We needed to give our children the tools they needed to find healthy foods.

We already grow a lot of our food, and our daughters love our annual garden. For the last several years, they have asked for their own garden beds, and our teen has started having a theme. One year, she grew a Zombie Garden, using plants that are used to fight the invading zombies in the video game Plants vs. Zombies. Her garden bed included sunflowers, peas, potatoes and pumpkins. Another year, we scoured the seed catalog for plants with animal names, like green panther cauliflower and deer tongue lettuce. Our daughters also love collecting eggs from the chickens and ducks in the backyard, raising chickens for the freezer every year and boiling sap for maple syrup.

It is not that our daughters do not know good food when they see it. They know what a real baby carrot is, how beets grow and what potato plants look like. They know apples grow on trees and raspberries do not. They know peas, pumpkins and cucumbers all grow on vines. They know they can eat some flowers and that once some plants start to flower, they can no longer be eaten.

They know about food, but like other kids their ages, they have also enjoyed the fact of our modern life — that some food does not look like other food, and it comes in a box. The "easy to get food," the "always there when we are hungry food," comes from the store. Unfortunately, more and more, the stuff that ends up being labeled food is not really safe to eat.

I could hear my daughter's unspoken question in her tears: if you are telling me that I cannot eat the food from the grocery store, and I trust what you are saying, then, what can I eat?

I realized that we needed an easy-to-find alternative to what is offered at our supermarket.

We live in a cold climate with a short growing season and the belief that there is very little available to eat when the trees are bare. With that in mind, we are always on the lookout for wild things that could be eaten when nothing else is growing. In addition, as our comfort level with wild edibles has grown, so too has our interest in discovering what our native ancestors ate. We began to ask ourselves that question — what did people who lived in North America eat before there were grocery stores and food imports? Obviously, they ate something, and unlike much of what we find in our modern grocery stores, most of what they ate did not have the potential to cause long-term systemic damage. As our interest in wild edibles and seasonal diets increased, we were encouraged to discover their secrets.

So, that day in the woods hunting for chaga, when I saw the greens poking through the leaf litter, I thought this plant must be a green that wildlife eats during the winter. It did not really occur to me that it might be something I could eat, but rather, it was a simple up-the-food-chain train of thought. The animals eat the green stuff, our ancestors ate the animals.

"You think?" he said, bending over to pick one of the leaves.

"Not 'wintergreen,'" I corrected. "A winter 'green.' You know, something that stays green during winter."

He snapped the leaf in half and smelled it.

"Are you sure?" he asked, holding the leaf to my nose.

The pungent sweet odor of wintergreen filled my olfactory senses, and I smiled. We had discovered wintergreen (*Gaultheria procumbens*) — a plant that grows during the winter, in our cold climate, and is indeed edible (as a tea, and the berries can also be eaten and are delicious).

Encouraged by our discovery and the knowledge that we seemed to be developing a kind of intuitive sense about the plant life around us, we decided to make a plan to be more proactive about looking for wild foods. Like many best-laid-plans, our mundane, day-to-day suburban life interfered, and not a lot happened.

And then ...

As if Fate had heard our dilemma and decided to give us a break, my mother sent us a box of books. While our family members do not always understand or agree with how we have chosen to live (they think we are kind of fun and quirky, mostly), they try to indulge our interests. As it turns out, my aunt and her late husband were prolific writers during the 1970s, and many of their books were about wild and medicinal edibles.

In the box were several books written by my aunt and uncle, including one that would lead us on the adventure of our lives. In answer to our unspoken request to the Universe, we were gifted a copy of the 1974 edition of *A Naturalist's Guide to Cooking with Wild Plants* by Connie and Arnold Krochmal.[1]

When I first saw it in the box, I figured it was just another book about collecting wild edibles, the kind with extensive and complicated preparation instructions and cautions about eating wild foods. So, I put it in a pile of books to be perused at a later date and promptly forgot about it, as my life took its typical twists and turns.

I placed my Johnny Seed order. We started harvesting maple syrup. The chickens started laying again. In general, we prepared for spring on our nanofarm, with some intention of, probably, eventually, as time allowed, getting out into the woods and wild foraging for some delicacies, when we wanted a change of pace. As with other

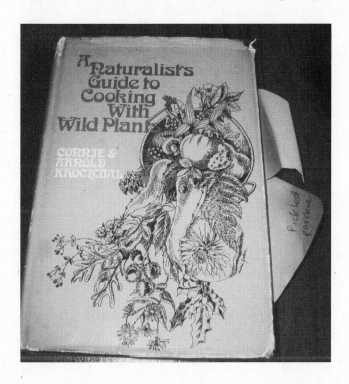

years, the focus would be on what we could grow (i.e., control) right on our quarter acre.

As Willy Wonka proclaims, "The best prize is a surprise."

A few weeks after the box arrived, I was prodded into taking a closer look at the books, and as I shuffled through the stack, the cookbook caught my eye. I started flipping through the pages. The foods are listed in alphabetical order, and so acorn was first. We had some experience with acorns, and while we had harvested and prepped acorns in one of our outdoor skills classes, we had not successfully turned them to flour on our own. Indeed, the whole process was very daunting, and since we were not really sure how to eat the acorn flour once we made it, we postponed practicing the skill.

I read through the processing instructions and scanned the acorn recipes. So simple. So straightforward. I was intrigued, and flipping the pages, I started to get a little excited. By the time I had reached the c's, I was giddy.

Of the first sixteen plants featured in the book, ten of them grew in my area, and not only that, but *I could identify them*. Ten plants I could identify. Edible ... and the best part about the cookbook — it has incredibly simple recipes using ingredients that are easily acquired and usually found in the average kitchen — salt, butter, flour, eggs, milk, sugar, oil, vinegar.

And better, most of those added ingredients are things we have made (vinegar and butter), we raise (eggs) and/or come from a local farmer (milk and lard, as a substitute for cooking oil) or are things we can produce from our foraging efforts (flour).

I have long maintained that there is no reason for the average person to be hungry. Plenty of food, free for the taking, grows unassisted and unhindered in the wild spaces where most of us fear to tread (except with our fully stocked and accessorized backpacks).

Many years ago, during a camping trip with some friends, I noticed an apple tree in the middle of the campground. We walked by it several times a day on our way to the bathroom. Although, at the time, I did not know much about anything, especially wild foods, the apples were clearly apples, and given the number on the ground around the tree, and the fact that it was late September, those apples were ready to harvest. Given the fullness of the tree and the sheer number of drops, it was also pretty clear that no one was harvesting it. So, I did, gathering as many as I could carry (while the rest of my group plodded back to our campsite).

For dinner that night, I cooked the apples with some of the oatmeal we had brought, a bit of sugar and butter and some water. It was delicious, and I quipped that we should go camping sometime and forage all of our food. My friend immediately nixed my idea as being ridiculous and undoable.

"No way! We would starve," she declared.

Over the years, I have learned how wrong her belief is, in spite of the fact that it is the prevailing attitude. Armed with my aunt's book and a growing knowledge of wild edibles, we embarked on the adventure of eating the wild food that shared our suburban environment.

This book is the story of our experiences through our seasons of eating free from nature's bounty.

We divided the book into three sections:

Part I: What We Did

This section describes what we did. We start by discussing the decision to make a very concerted effort, over a calendar year, of incorporating foraged foods into our diet and setting some goals for ourselves. Then we describe the kinds of plants that we actually foraged, how we ate them and how we preserved them (many of the foods we foraged did end up as stored foods, and learning to store food for the winter was a big part of the project).

Part II: Why We Decided to Start Foraging

This section focuses on our growing concerns about the safety, availability and cost of grocery store food, which played a pretty significant role in our desire to adopt foraging as a way of life rather than just a once-in-awhile hobby.

Part III: Life Lessons We Learned from Foraging

Our foraging adventure was not just about going out and finding food. It was about a lot of things, including changing our very definition of food. Not only did we have to learn about specific plants, but we also had to learn how to use them to nourish our bodies and how to prepare them into foods that would be both aesthetically appealing and palatable.

Along the way, we learned some very important facts about the nature of food and of, well, *nature*. Our culture has allowed us to become completely complacent about our food. We make a grocery list and then pick up what we need. As we learned, nature does not work that way, and often what one hopes to find is not there, and if it was there last week, it may not be next week.

We learned five specific lessons and discuss each one as it applied to our foraging efforts.

We are not expert foragers by any stretch of the imagination, and this book is not a how-to guide for foraging. It is a story, peppered with a few interesting ways to cook some common *wild* foods, but mostly it is about taking control and regaining our freedom.

Part I

What We Did

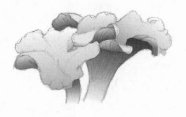

CHAPTER 1

Goals

GRIEF IS AN EMOTIONAL RESPONSE ONE EXPERIENCES when one suffers a loss. Most often we associate grief with death, and indeed, when we first learned the term "peak oil," there was a huge feeling of loss, or impending loss, for half of our duo.

Our initial responses to learning the implications of peak oil were very different. With the understanding that, without oil, everything we depended on for our lives (not just lifestyle, but just to be alive) would be at best scarce and/or incredibly expensive, Wendy went into a full-blown panic mode. The biggest concern was how to feed ourselves if food from the grocery store was not available.

The five stages of grief are usually described as: denial, anger, bargaining, depression and acceptance. While some may experience linear movement through the stages, most often they are, to some degree, overlapping, and some stages may not be experienced in the order listed above. Typically, however, those experiencing grief will touch on all five at some point in the process. Although acceptance is seen as the last stage, when it comes to the loss of our lifestyles and the continued degradation of the planet, after acceptance there needs to be an action.

Wendy's response to peak oil was two-fold. First was the resolution to grow as much as possible on our quarter acre. Garden beds were constructed on every available inch of our lot, and suggestions for expanding the potential garden space included using the fence for trellising plants or espaliering fruit trees, hanging planters from the eaves and building frames over the raised beds so that buckets could be suspended over the in-the-ground garden. Every now and then, some suggestion about planting on the leach-field was presented, and the roof of our house was even considered as a prime location for more garden space.

Regular trips to the local nurseries resulted in adding to our food production with a couple of apple trees, an enviable herb garden and berry brambles. Techniques like espaliering fruit trees have been heavily researched and tried.

Books on organic gardening techniques, container gardening, suburban gardening, small-space gardening and forest gardening began to fill the shelves. Magazines, like *Mother Earth News* and *Organic Gardener*, became bathroom reading material. The Internet was scoured, sometimes for hours and at the expense of other activities, for suggestions and advice on how to make our lot more productive.

Because we are meat eaters, laying hens and ducks were given a home in our backyard, and they have kept us in eggs, and for the past many years, we have devoted our summer to raising meat chickens. Rabbits have always been a part of our homestead. There was some unsuccessful cajoling related to a desire to add goats (for milk, fiber and meat) to what was beginning to resemble a teeny farm.

In just a few years, we went from growing a few tomatoes and cucumbers to a real working homestead, and our food production numbers went through the roof.

But we were still not producing all of the food we needed, and so the second option was to become fully entrenched in the local foods movement. The mantra became, *If it doesn't grow in Maine, we don't eat it.*

During all of this time, Eric remained quietly calm and just kept repeating, "We do not need to grow all of our food." Wendy disagreed, and in her fear and desperation, she did not hear the real message. What she heard was something to the effect that her efforts to grow enough food for a family of five on a quarter-acre suburban lot were a ridiculous waste of time (and nicknames like "Fundy Wendy" that were occasionally bandied about did not help to clear up any misunderstandings). It was not that Eric thought it could not be done, but rather that he thought it was not necessary, and the only thing Wendy was hearing was that "not necessary" part. The message she missed was not that we should not garden, but that if we just stopped and looked around, there was plenty of food, provided for free by nature.

We have been fascinated by wilderness survival for a long time but had never applied it in any practical sense. When things got slow, we would occasionally peruse one of our dozens of books about edible or medicinal plants. We collected and hungrily devoured videos featuring survival experts like Ray Mears, but as far as actually taking the time to get outside and identify, harvest and use plants as food or medicine, we too often found that our plates were too full of those mundane activities of suburban life. As such, our interest and desire to know about those plants were relegated to fond dreams for the future.

Having convinced herself that a quarter acre was more than adequate land for growing all the food a typical suburban family of five would need to subsist, Wendy spent countless hours turning our formerly sterile suburban lot into a lush, edible jungle. She was certain that by putting the right plants in the right spot at the right time our goals would be met. Eric knew, but his ever logical and concise engineer brain was unable to articulate the understanding that, with or without the constant, backbreaking toil of the garden, food would grow.

Native American tribes had flourished all over the country, even in the inhospitable climate of southern Maine. There is a great deal of evidence, with more fascinating archeological data being unearthed all of the time, showing that these large cultures thrived for thousands of years with nothing more than their understanding of the land and its gifts. Modern Americans, indeed most of us living in this global society today, have lost the knowledge and the skills our ancestors had that enabled them to work with the plants that grow freely around us. While Wendy was busy trying to cultivate carrots, Eric knew that if we could relearn even just a little of this knowledge, coupled with what we could grow on our little lot, we would not have to worry about food security and safety.

At some point, we realized that we had the same worries, and if our solutions were just a bit different, they did not contradict, but rather complemented.

If we were to look back over the last several years to find that exact moment when the idea of foraging went from *not gonna happen* to *let's do it*, we would not be able to say it was this day or that. Further, if we tried to find a single event that motivated us to adopt a foraging lifestyle/mindset, we would be pretty hard-pressed to pinpoint it. More accurately, we would say that it was a series of small steps, like going up the steep sides of one of those South American monuments. One step and another, and taking some time in between for a breather. In short, there was no epiphany followed by our rushing out and starting to dig up dandelion roots for a coffee substitute. It took us some time, and we had to overcome a lot of mistaken notions and cultural biases before we got to where we are.

At first, we just started noticing plants that seemed to be prolific in our area. One would catch our attention, and we decided to figure out what it was. The first ones were easy — berries. They are pretty much a no-brainer, and honestly, we have both been foraging wild blackberries since we were little, playing with our friends in our suburban wildernesses. In some ways, it was like eating forbidden fruit. We never told anyone about our find, nor did we bring home foraged bounty to share, as there was some unspoken idea that what we were doing would not be met with any enthusiasm. Most suburban moms are not terribly amenable to the idea that their little ones were eating stuff found on the sides of the roads or out in the woods.

What is great about berries is that, whatever the variety, they are pretty much the same regardless of locale. Blackberries in Maine are the same blackberries we picked as kids in Alabama or as teens in Kentucky. Growing up we never knew anyone who cultivated blackberries. Until we planted berry brambles, those kinds of berries were always wild ... or something from the store that were cultivated at some magical place where grocery store food was grown, by experts who knew about making sure the food is absolutely safe, perfect and delicious (it can be interesting how we perceive food production when we simply do not take the time to think about it).

After we discovered wild blackberries, we branched out to making teas from things like sweet fern (*Comptonia peregrina*) and pine needles. In fact, sweet fern was one of the first plants we taught our daughters to identify.

The more we learned, the more we wanted to know, but it was still just identifying a plant here or a plant there, and not ever really knowing much more than what can be used as a tea or has an edible root. We muddled along, continuing to notice things. Most of our knowledge started as simple observation followed by a flurry of research through books and the Internet.

We took a few outdoor skills classes that included plant identification and actually learned uses for some of them. We purchased more books, including Thomas Elpel's *Botany in a Day: The Patterns Method of Plant Identification*, which, instead of focusing on individual plants, teaches identification on a family basis.[1]

Then one day, we noticed a weird plant, not something we had planted, growing in our forest garden. Since we had often had wonderful luck with volunteers, we let it grow, which it did. When the plant was two feet high, we noticed little berry-like growths that looked a lot like teeny-tiny tomatoes.

"It's not a tomato," Wendy said. "The leaves are wrong."

Then, as an afterthought, queried aloud, "Maybe it's a member of the nightshade family."

Both potatoes and tomatoes are nightshades. Night lantern, a vine with very distinctive purple and yellow flowers that mature into bright red fruits, is also a member, and all three grow in our yard. The mystery plant seemed to have some similar qualities.

Using nightshade as a starting point, we discovered the plant was Eastern Black Nightshade (*Solanum ptychanthum*). As with all other members, the green leafy parts are inedible. Many, like Night lantern, also have an inedible berry. According to the information we found, the unripe berry of the Eastern Black Nightshade (the green ones) are poisonous but edible when they mature and go black.

While there was no single catalyst, little things, like discovering Eastern Black Nightshade, caused a shift. We had not planted this, but the seeds had to have come from somewhere, close enough that they were carried to our yard. We decided to embark on a journey of discovery and growth by expanding our meager foraging knowledge, and to motivate ourselves to really follow through, we decided to make it a project.

The project we outlined was simple: we wanted to find out what was in our local environment that we could eat. From the beginning, we knew that different plants appeared at different times throughout the year. As fledgling foragers, we also had to keep our expectations realistic. Because we needed a way to measure our progress and to focus our efforts, we set some simple goals to guide us. They would also motivate us to learn new plants beyond those we already knew. Our goals were:

1. Harvest one item to eat with a meal each week, even if only as a side dish or an ingredient in a larger dish (like quiche);
2. Learn to store anything that we could not consume;
3. Keep track of the amount of food (by weight) that we foraged and attempt to match our foraged food totals with our cultivated food totals;

4. Host a party at the end of the summer, the menu to include, primarily, foraged foods.

One of our objectives was to see how many different foods we could gather and how much of each. To record our progress, we also kept track of the foods by weight.

Before we could fully begin the project, however, we needed to clearly define what we meant by "foraging," because as soon as we started getting into it, we realized that there could be some very broad interpretations of the word. First, for us, it did not include any food that had ever been in a package. Our basic definition of foraging, therefore, started with the assumption that the food we were seeking was either rooted in the ground or living without human intervention.

Then, we started asking questions about location. For instance, if the food was growing in our yard but we did not plant it, could that be considered a foraged food? If the food were anywhere on or around developed land, could it be considered a wild food? Because we are based in the suburbs, getting away from land that might have, at some point, been cultivated, would have been well-nigh impossible. Even the area woods were, in recent history, farmlands. We know this partly from anecdotal tales from our old-timer neighbors, but also by their nature, mostly populated by the fast-growing pines and poplars that are the first to appear when clear-cut land returns to nature.

To make things easier for us and to be sure that we were being consistent, we developed three criteria that our foraged food would have to satisfy:

- It must have grown without being purposely planted or raised by us or anyone we knew (meaning that non-native apple trees planted by some old farmer, counted as wild).
- It must have grown without human intervention … no watering, fertilizing, weeding, etc.
- It could, and did, include animal sources.

At first we thought of organizing the project as had many of the "Our Year of ..." books that are available on everything from not buying stuff from China to eating local foods or spending a year going green. It is a familiar format, one that is very popular both for readers and writers. Readers can live vicariously through the authors; authors can dabble in a lifestyle one might not ordinarily live, knowing that it will end at a specified time.

But as the seasons blended one into the other, we realized that this project, this goal of incorporating wild foods into our lives, was a lot more about making deep, philosophical changes in ourselves. Trying to cook one meal per week or have an "all foraged" meal per month for any reason other than improving our lives began to feel contrived. Sometime during our quest for wild foods, we realized that the project was not about writing a book, as so many of the year-long pursuits ultimately seemed to be, but rather about changing our eating habits to include the foods that naturally grow locally. Very early on, we recognized that it would not be a simple year-long experiment to see if we could, but it would drastically change what and how we ate.

Through the growing season, we did manage to have one meal per week that included something foraged, and we even continued to eat foraged foods, at least once a week, into the winter, thanks to storing some portion of them — even if we just made a cup of tea from foraged nettles. In August 2012, we hosted our Second Annual Brown Family Summer Party, serving several dishes that featured foraged foods, as promised. We harvested, ate and stored dozens of plants we had previously only been moderately acquainted with — learning to identify and use them, and even to make meals that complemented the stronger or different flavors.

At some point, the project became more about how we wanted to live than about recording the experience as an experiment — one in which we might retain some lesson or some habit, but at the end we fully intended to return to our "normal" life. With the exception of spending more time than usual out in the woods, for the most part, foraging did not change the way we lived our lives. We still did all of the other things we always do, only we were learning some pretty cool stuff, getting some exercise and exploring our local environment just a little more. We also noticed that when we were in less familiar places, we would start looking for plants we knew from home. The activity of foraging was incorporated into our lives rather than taking the place of something else we would have otherwise been doing.

We met and exceeded the goals we set when we decided to try foraging for a year. This is a journal of our efforts, what we foraged, why we wanted to in the first place and what we learned in the process. It chronicles our triumphs and our less-than-successful endeavors; thankfully there were many examples of both.

We still have a lot to learn, and we are eager for future growing seasons that will find us out, browsing nature's aisles in search of wild foods.

CHAPTER 2

Greens

ALTHOUGH OUR PROJECT BEGAN IN THE FALL/WINTER TIME, we began to get very excited in the early spring. This project is something that we had talked about for a while, but the cold reality is that there is little to forage once the snow lies on the ground here in Maine. A few things can be gathered, such as evergreen boughs and tassels for tea, or the inner bark of several trees, which can be used in stews or dried and pounded into flour. In spring, after the snow has melted, the ground warms and life stirs again; there is new growth with its life-giving nutrition.

Once the snow has cleared, a few plants are ready for foraging, but they offer little substantial nutritional value. These would definitely present those relying on the ability to hunt and gather a glimmer of hope and an assurance that nature would once again share her bounty. The spring really comes into focus for us with the reddening of the red maple branches and the maple sugaring season.

One food that is ready for harvest as soon as the snow melts is wintergreen. In fact, the berries live through the winter under the snow cover. Although not filling, they are a sure sign that nature has provided. For some species of forest animals, these beautiful red

berries offer the first food in spring. For me, they are a delightful opportunistic nibble that gives me a chance to commune with the world around us. Fittingly, I found these berries while I was out gathering wood for the fire to boil maple syrup.

As soon as the taps stopped flowing and the sap was stored in jars of sweet amber syrup, we began looking in earnest for other things to harvest. Our first trip out into the woods was too early for foraging any tasty morsels, but the trip was not without reward. While we did not have any foraged foods to grace our table, we had a new understanding of what was starting to grow and where to find the plants we hoped to eat.

Each year, our garden is filled with a number of different greens, common in many home gardens, like leaf lettuces, spinach, kale and braising mixes. We enjoy them all in stir-fries and salads during the season, and some will end up as dehydrated mixed greens for adding to soups during the winter.

In our small yard, we successfully grow a rather large diversity of plants. We decided very early after purchasing our property and starting to plant gardens that we would buy perennials only if they were either edible or medicinal. We have expanded the rule to include only edible annuals. As such, while we enjoy flowers as much as the next person, only those from medicinal or edible plants adorn our garden spaces. The nasturtiums grown in the tower of old tires were a delicious, peppery addition to a greens salad.

Even with all of the raised beds we have built and the container gardens, there is simply not enough space to produce everything to satisfy our dietary needs. As such, we began looking to foraging to help fill this gap.

While we grow what could be considered some nutritional powerhouses of cultivated greens, we found that, during the course of our project, the wild greens were actually the more reliable food source for two reasons. First, the wild greens grew unaided and unimpeded by us, requiring nor wanting anything from us, including prepping a bed and adding seeds. Second, sometimes the cultivated greens grew, and we could pick and eat them. Other times, they did not grow — either the seeds were not viable (due to a low germination rate), or the weather was not friendly to that seed. Wild greens are not that persnickety; they grow whether we notice or not. They may not be exactly where we expect to find them, but usually they are not terribly far away.

We had quite a few greens in mind that we wished to try and had a pretty good idea of where they were. On our first, questionably unsuccessful trip out into the woods and nearby fields, we confirmed that they would be available.

Stinging nettles (*Urtica dioica*) was one of the first plants we sought. A good-sized patch was in the field near our house. In early April, we visited it a few times before it had grown large enough to pick the tender young leaves. The first harvest of nettles was modest, filling only the bottom of a small basket.

We added the nettles to one of our first harvest meals, which included smoked chicken, Japanese knotweed (*Fallopia japonica*) and Jerusalem artichoke (*Helianthus tuberosus*) sautéed with butter and garlic. This simple dish was incredibly nutritious and delightfully delicious.

Even though the initial harvest was not very big, we did not use all of the nettles as a side dish. The remainder was dehydrated. Over the spring and early summer, we returned several times to the nettles patch to harvest these vitamin-packed leaves for dehydrating to be enjoyed during our long Maine winter.

Like many of the plants we hoped to enjoy over the course of our foraging adventure, we discovered that we were often competing with nature, and too often losing. When we went back in early July to find a few more nettles to ensure that we had enough for the

Stinging nettles.

coming winter, we discovered that the patch had been ravaged. All that was left was the bare branches. Every leaf had been stripped bare.

The mild weather at the beginning of the year had provided ideal conditions for the Red Admiral butterflies to reproduce in record numbers and remain further north that winter than is usual. As we discovered, nettles are a favorite food, and they enjoyed every bit of the patch that we had come to think of as our own private store. It was a disappointing blow.

As it turns out, however, it provided quite a few valuable lessons. First, nature works in cycles. If there is an abundance of a certain species, nature will compensate. Because there were so many nettles in this field, the butterflies came to feast. This they did with no regard for anything else dependent on these stinging nettles. But nature is also resilient, and while the plants looked devastated, really, it was just the same leafy parts that we wanted for our winter stores. The roots and stalks were still intact. Once the butterflies had mated and laid their eggs, the nettles recovered.

The dried nettle leaves are not just used as a tea. Early in the season, we labeled an old pickle jar "Soup Greens," and over the course of our foraging summer, we dehydrated these and other greens, including dandelions, that would add flavor and a vitamin-packed boost to the broth of soups and stews over our cold winter. As the contents of the jar slowly disappeared, we resolved to be more diligent about finding these vitamin powerhouses during the next growing season.

For any plant, a single use, such as the soup greens, is sufficient to prove its worth for foragers. These offer a flavor that we will be unable to find fresh in the wild for several more months.

Dandelions, however, have more uses than just this one. The leaves can also be used fresh cut from the plant. Throughout the summer, we added them to a mixed greens salad, often topping the dish with a few flowers for added color and flavor. Both wild and cultivated

Dandelion flowers in bloom.

flowers have adorned our salads, and two favorites are violets (wild) and nasturtiums (homegrown).

Our antics often amuse the neighbors, who have come to expect and accept something different from us. There are times, though, that we still surprise them. One morning after seeing me gathering wild greens in the uncultivated edges of our yard for a salad for lunch at work, one neighbor stopped to inquire — in jest — if I was making a salad for lunch. I imagine the neighbor was probably quite surprised by my affirmative reply.

Back in the late 70s and early 80s, there was a very popular inventor of kitchen gadgets named Ron Popeil. His products were often featured on half-hour-long commercials (dubbed infomercials), and on some days, with little else to watch, we would spend that half hour learning all of the wonderful ways Mr. Popeil's products would benefit our lives. Every single infomercial always included the words,

"But wait! There's more!" because there was always one more great way that the product could be used. It was never just a juicer/blender; it could also make ice cream!

Dandelion greens were like that for us. We ate them raw in salads, we sautéed them in butter and garlic for a tasty side dish, and we dehydrated them for use later in winter soups and stews. We also enjoyed the later greens, when the leaves are larger and not quite so sweet (if dandelion greens could ever be considered sweet), when most people have given up eating them because they have become bitter.

We discovered that the late greens are wonderful as a substitute for the very strongly flavored basil in pesto. If nothing else can be said about us, one has to concede that we are not afraid of experimenting with recipes to tweak them so that they will work with what we have on hand. We printed a basic pesto recipe, scanned the ingredients and got to work making substitutions.

First, we traipsed out into the yard and, in a section that is not visited by the dog or the chickens, snipped a handful of enormous dandelion leaves that grew, unassisted and unmolested, in the forest garden under the Granny Smith apple tree. To this bundle, we added some mint leaves and garlic scapes, because the garlic scapes were ready for harvest, but the bulbs underground were not quite formed — and we needed a way to use the garlic scapes, too. Everything else required for the pesto was in the kitchen.

Pesto is actually pretty simple. It has five basic ingredients: garlic, an herb, olive oil, nuts and salt. By late spring, our winter garlic stores are used up, and whether a function of good planning or good luck, the stalks on the garlic bulbs planted the previous fall are usually huge and beautiful, and the scapes are curly. Some gardening sources recommend cutting the scapes before they straighten out if a larger bulb is desired. They have the same wonderful garlic flavor as the bulbs, and not wanting to waste anything that we could use as food, we used the scapes for our dandelion pesto experiment.

The herbs were the dandelion greens (ten or so very large leaves — more than half had veins as big around as a pencil — and mint leaves. Pine nuts come from pine trees, and while Maine is the Pine Tree State, the varieties with nuts large enough to even bother harvesting are not native to our area. Instead we added roasted and salted pumpkin seeds, which are widely available throughout New England.

We put the garlic scapes in the food processer, added the herbs and drizzled in some olive oil, whizzing everything until it was all chopped up. Then, not liking the consistency, we added a bit more olive oil and the nuts and salt. Because the texture was a little more creamy than desired, we added more dandelion greens, but they tempered the garlic a little more than we liked, and so we added another garlic scape and more olive oil. After all of the tweaking and additional ingredients, the dandelion pesto was actually quite tasty, and not bitter at all. We were surprised by how delicious it actually was, and served over pasta as an accompaniment to one of our homegrown chickens, it created a delectable meal.

As Ron Popeil would have said, "But wait! There's more!" although dandelion greens are amazing, they are not the only aerial parts of the plant to enjoy. The flowers are edible and can be battered and fried making dandelion flower fritters, which if we were more fond of deep-fried cooking would have become a family favorite. Dandelion flowers can also be made into wine, and with our very strong interest in brewing, dandelion wine will certainly find its way into our foraging repertoire at some point.

Plantain, like dandelion, is another common weed in our area that has a few useful parts. We eat the leaves as an early green in salads. Later in the summer, the bigger leaves tend to be tough and stringy, and so we do not pick them if they are more than two inches across. In addition, the seeds can be used as grain, which can be gathered, dried and ground into flour.

We have discovered that many of our favorite plants, as well as being edible, have medicinal qualities. Plantain can be an effective cure for skin irritation caused by stinging nettles. While being able to put acquired knowledge into practice is often desired, sometimes we like to learn without having the experience. Learning how well plantain worked against stinging nettles, it turns out, is something we would rather have continued to know in theory rather than practice.

One day, our granddaughter came foraging with us. As we waded through the, to her, knee-high grasses, a stinging nettles leaf brushed against her hand and immediately resulted in an angry red rash with raised white blotches. She burst into tears from the pain of the sting. Quick-thinking grandpa found some plantain leaves, which were quickly masticated into a poultice and applied to the rash.

We resolved to go back home, but even before we had made it the hundred yards out of the field to the path in the woods that lead back to our house, her sobs had stopped. By the time we got home (a ten-minute walk), there was no evidence of the rash. We made sure to point out both of these amazing plants to her so that she would recognize both the cause of the rash and one of the cures.

The suburban landscape, having vast swaths of waste and little-used spaces, is a treasure trove of edible possibilities for those who know to look. Many of the greens we enjoy grow in these waste areas, including one of our favorites, the common violet (*Viola odorata*).

Violets are another weed that grows with abandon along the road that borders our yard. We watched as they grew from tiny little buds right through beyond the flowering stage. The tender young leaves became salad ingredients with the dandelion and plantain leaves. The small leaves are also enjoyed just as a nibble when we walk by them. The delicate little flowers that grow fairly early in the season can be a fun, quick snack, but the lovely purple blossoms also add a wonderful color and flavor to salads.

We ate most of our harvested greens raw in salads, and had a lot of fun experimenting with different types, both wild and cultivated. On the Fourth of July, we made a salad we called "Fireworks Salad" because we added nasturtium flowers in bright reds, oranges and yellows, which looked like exploding fireworks. The salad also contained dandelion leaves, violet leaves, violet flowers and some cultivated greens from the garden.

Even before we started our foraging adventure, we ate locally and in season, and after a long winter of stored foods, our bodies craved greens. Appropriately, greens are one of the first foraged foods we find as winter loosens its icy grip on our landscape.

As we reflect on our year of foraging adventures, one thing we marvel at is nature's capacity to heal, and while we cannot prove it (yet — more research definitely needs to be done), we are certain that the foods nature offers at any given time of the year are exactly the foods we need to achieve optimal health. That is, what grows where we live is what we need to stay healthy.

The fireworks salad was as eye-pleasing as it was palate-pleasing.

Dandelion Pesto

8 to 10 large dandelion leaves
2 cloves garlic or six garlic scapes
¼ cup roasted and salted pumpkin seeds
⅔ cup extra-virgin olive oil
Salt, to taste
Optional: ½ cup freshly grated hard cheese (like Parmesan or Romano)

1. Place dandelion leaves and pumpkin seeds in blender and pulse until coarsely chopped.
2. Add garlic (over-processing the garlic can make the pesto taste a bit too strong) and pulse until coarsely chopped.
3. Add olive oil and process until fully incorporated and smooth. Add salt to taste.

* I intended to freeze whatever wasn't used, so I did not add the cheese. This can be added later or left out. It is good either way.

CHAPTER 3

Roots And Shoots

SOMETIME DURING THE DEEP FREEZE OF WINTER, when the world is gray and white, we are teased with catalogs of brightly colored fruits and vegetables to be gained if we just buy this seed or that, and we succumb to the temptation every year, planning what we want to eat next winter and buying our seeds. In the spring, as soon as possible, we begin to work the soil (and there have been years when we were, indeed, scooping snow off the top of our heavily mulched beds to loosen the thawing soil underneath). For us, gardening is, to use a cliché, a crap shoot. Some years the stars all align, and everything we plant sprouts, buds and blooms right on schedule, and we have an abundant harvest with lots of fresh treats from the garden and plenty to store. Some years, not so much. If we had to depend on our garden, we would be in trouble, and it took more time than it should have to come to the realization that we do not have to be dependent on the garden — or the grocery store.

One cherished crop is the annual planting of potatoes. These beloved and well-known roots are a staple in our diet over the winter, and we know we need at least a hundred pounds to get us through the cold. We eat them in stews, baked, roasted and mashed, grated and fried into hash, boiled and even as a soup. To increase our yield, we have tried several techniques, including planting a whole raised bed with just potatoes and using several different types of containers. The results have been mixed, and not always terribly productive. We have never come close to achieving the needed hundred pounds, and usually supplement our meager harvest with potatoes from a local farm store, where we buy fifty pound bags.

After so many disappointing harvests, we turned our sights to other roots, and we discovered Jerusalem artichokes (*Helianthus tuberosus*), also known as sunchokes. Several features of sunchokes make them preferable to potatoes. First, they are far superior nutritionally, because they contain very high amounts of iron, and they are one of the finest sources of dietary fibers, and inulin, which makes them an ideal sweetener for diabetics.[1]

More importantly, though, is that, sunchokes are indigenous to the northeastern United States, unlike potatoes that are indigenous to South America. Natives reportedly planted them along the rivers, where they grew, because that is exactly what sunchokes do best, as any gardener who has welcomed them into his garden can attest. Sunchokes grow, and grow and grow! The stalks reach as high as fifteen feet and, from that lofty height, sprout a tiny yellow flower that waves to us in slight breezes. Meanwhile, underground, one tiny piece of root will produce a half-dozen offspring. A patch we planted on a hill started out with twelve roots, and by the end of the summer, covered the entire hill and spilled into the road. They do not seem to be terribly picky with regard to the type of soil, whether rich with organic matter or thin sand replete with winter salts, and we are fairly certain that the sunchokes would grow right across the dirt road if they were not continually assaulted by the cars driving over them. It certainly provided a lesson in growing native plants that have thrived for centuries.

The sunchokes and potatoes we planted are certainly not wild foraged foods. Even though they are native to our area, we have yet to find sunchokes actually growing in the wild, and it is an interesting little mystery. Still, given the prolific nature of the plant, it has quickly overwhelmed us, and us being us, we have allowed it to simply take over — in essence, it has rewilded that portion of our yard. We do not water it. We do not fertilize it. We do not weed it. Our stand of sunchokes are not truly wild, but they are a semi-feral source of food for us in the fall and early spring.

The one reason that potatoes are preferable to sunchokes is the ability to store them for long periods. Sunchokes can not be stored for months in a root cellar. That said, sunchokes are wonderful dried and ground into flour, which adds a nutty, earthy flavor to winter foods. As most literature advises, the best way to store sunchokes is in the ground, dug as needed before the ground freezes. Given their mostly fresh diet, the natives who depended on sunchokes as a nutrient-dense energy food knew to dig the roots and eat them when they were harvested, rather than trying to store a winter's worth.

Not finding truly wild sunchokes is unfortunate, but there are other options for wild roots that we began to experiment with finding, and the sunchokes were actually a really good lesson on the nature of roots. As a gardener, one plants the potato and waits as the plant moves through its life cycle. When the aerial parts of the plant die back, the potato root, the part we eat, is ready to harvest. Other roots are similar. With sunchokes, in the fall, as the aerial parts of the plant are dying, the plant is putting its energy into its root where it is stored until the next spring. If one digs the sunchoke while the aerial parts are green and lush, the root will be mushy and inedible. Digging the late fall or early spring roots yields a hard, crispy potato-like tuber that is sweet and nutty and starchy — delicious eaten raw and just as palatable when cooked.

We learned from our sunchokes that roots are best harvested at two times when the rest of the plant is dormant — in the spring before the plant awakens and begins growing anew and in the fall after the rest of the plant above ground dies back.

An argument could be made for harvesting roots at either time. Digging the roots in the fall provides for better plant identification because the dead stems, leaves, shoots and flowers provide clues. Unearthing the roots in the spring encourages one to wake up with the rest of the natural world and to start watching for new plants to forage. Leaving roots in the ground preserves them for the spring but makes it difficult to gather if food supplies run short in winter.

We have not developed a preference for one season or the other for digging roots. Being still rather new to foraging as a whole, we dug most of the roots we sampled in the fall, because we had the dying foliage to help identify the location. As novice foragers, we only harvest what we can positively identify.

One of the first wild root crops that we recognized was wild carrot (also known as Queen Anne's Lace, or *Daucus carota*), which is widely considered a weed and likes to grow in all kinds of disturbed soils. The large clusters of flowers make it fairly easy to recognize, although there are a few poisonous plants that look like wild carrot. As we were taught, the key to successful foraging is to take advantage of all of our senses. How does the plant look: the color of the leaves (deep green, spotted), the way the leaves grow on the stem, the shape and size of the leaves? How does the plant feel: smooth, hairy, sticky, dry? What does the plant smell like? Look at the plant, feel the plant and note the texture, smell the plant and remember the odor. We learned that true wild carrot, unlike the poisonous look-alikes, will smell like a carrot.

Our autodidactic ways often provide lessons in the form of failure. We tend to learn more completely and better through acting in ignorance. Nature is not a cruel teacher, exactly, but has little patience for careless stupidity. Luckily, wild carrots were one of the very few failures we had expanding our foraging efforts.

We tried harvesting wild carrots on a couple of occasions, most markedly in advance of our summer party, where we hoped to include them in the menu. Like sunchokes, however, there are good times to harvest wild carrots and not good times. We should have known this, but occasionally we still slip right back into that on-demand mindset, where carrots are always available, any time of year, usually machine-whittled into bite-sized nuggets and wrapped in plastic. All we needed to do to have carrots at our party was to correctly identify the plant and dig the roots.

Determined to find exactly what our taste buds demanded, a day or two before the party, we picked some wild carrots at a local land trust area. These were too tough to eat, and still it never occurred to us that the problem was not the carrots, but us being stupid. Undaunted by the tough carrots we had found at Indian Jane rock, we headed back through our woods to the field in search of an edible carrot. We were going to have carrots! But those we found in the field were also woody and too tough to eat ... try as we might.

Carrots, wild or otherwise, are biennials. The first year they concentrate on growing their root. They have a small green top above ground, but they will not flower the first year. Gardeners are familiar with the aerial parts of carrots. The next year, the carrot will put all of its energy into growing the aerial parts in preparation for making seeds. The second-year wild carrot plant produces the familiar Queen Anne's lace flower head (and to be completely sure that wild carrot is what you have, check the stems to see if they are "hairy," as some sources recommend the mnemonic device "Queen Anne has hairy legs"), and when the flowers die, the seeds are produced. When hell-bent on getting wild carrot, we used the flower heads as identification.

With wild carrot, the first-year roots are delicious, every bit the familiar taste of their cultivated cousins (albeit not orange). As the plant dedicates its second year to making seeds, the roots become woody and inedible. The folly of this whole deal is that we have grown carrot and knew all of this, but we did not even think to pick the first-year plants like those we have grown in our own garden in past years. It was a good lesson.

We did not make the same mistake with burdock (*Articum*), which is a biennial like carrot, although we did not find it until the fall when the leaves were dying back. Although we knew how to identify the plant, we had not planned to seek it out for harvesting. Our approach throughout this particular project was to gather what we found and could identify. One day while out gathering a list of plants that, from the walk the week before, we knew were ready, we stumbled upon the opportunity to harvest some of the tender first-year roots. As a matter of fact, we were finished for the day and walking back to the path to leave when Wendy spied it. She stopped, lovingly coaxed the root from the ground and dropped it into the basket with the rest of the haul.

At home, we carefully washed the root, sliced it up and added it to a stir-fry with some of the other plants we foraged that day. The experience with burdock was all very brief and impromptu. The stir-fry was likewise short-lived ... and delicious.

While we experimented with a lot of different and many new-to-us wild foods, one that turned out to be quite a delightful surprise was one of those that we kept intending to try, but never got around to harvesting. It was also one of the easiest to find and harvest, because it grew wild right in our yard.

For many years, we had heard and read about using dandelion root as a coffee substitute, but in our busy lives, it remained one of those pieces of untested knowledge. We had no direct experience with dandelion root. This year, we changed from being aware to really knowing, and we were completely thrilled to learn that:

- Dandelion root is incredibly healthful, especially as a beverage; and
- Roasted dandelion root, when ground into a powder and steeped in water, tastes just like coffee — at least to us, former heavy coffee drinkers.

Dandelion root is renowned for its blood-building properties, is high in iron and, as a coffee substitute, is caffeine free. What makes it particularly exciting for us is that we stopped drinking coffee some time ago and switched to tea, and have been transitioning from Asian-based *Camellia sinesis,* to herbal teas, because *Camellia sinesis,* from which green and black teas are derived, does not grow in Maine, in spite of our best efforts to grow it. Likewise, coffee beans are not hardy in our climate. It is quite a thrill to find a local plant (especially a wild one) that could be a substitute for these familiar but not locally available plants.

By contrast to some of the roots we sampled as opportunistic foragers, we actively sought out the roots of Japanese knotweed, and with those we did not make any amateurish blunders, like we did with the carrots. Japanese knotweed, an invasive, non-native species in our area, is often called "bamboo" and may have been introduced as a privacy screen. With no natural predators, it grows prolifically in our climate, and home gardeners will go to great lengths to eradicate it.

While Japanese knotweed root is not edible, it is medicinal. The roots contain the same health-promoting chemical, called *resveratrol,* as found in the skins of grapes, and because of the health benefits of this chemical, physicians and health care professionals are now recommending drinking a glass of wine for dinner. In Asia, the roots are used as a laxative.

In addition, new research is suggesting that it is useful in the treatment of Lyme disease, which, over the past many years, has reached almost epidemic proportions, especially in the northeastern United States. Plant experts, like Stephen Buhner (author of *Healing Lyme*),[2] suggest that the disease and associated symptoms are even more far-reaching than has been revealed by the medical establishment.

The one thing on which everyone agrees is that Lyme is transmitted to humans through tick bites, and in the outdoors classes that we have taken, we are always admonished to do a "tick check" when we get home. It is fairly common to hear that uttered around our house after walks, too. We decided to harvest the root for use as a prophylactic against Lyme.

Japanese knotweed likes to grow in waste areas and disturbed soils. Finding a clean spot is the first trick. Plants, especially roots, that are gathered for both food and medicine should only be harvested from "clean areas." The root is gathered in the fall, after the plants die back, and digging them up is no easy task. They tend to grow in all directions at once and down into the ground, some as deep as ten feet. They are gnarly and do not give up without a fight. The upside is that you can gather a large amount very quickly because of the size of the roots. Within an hour or so, we had harvested enough for an entire year.

Handling the roots should be done with care. As a piece of advice, clean the roots and cut them up into small pieces in the field. It probably cannot be said enough, but Japanese knotweed is incredibly invasive and, with ten-foot-deep tap roots, is extremely difficult to eradicate once it gets a foothold. Even the smallest piece of root, we were warned, can form a new stand in just a few years.

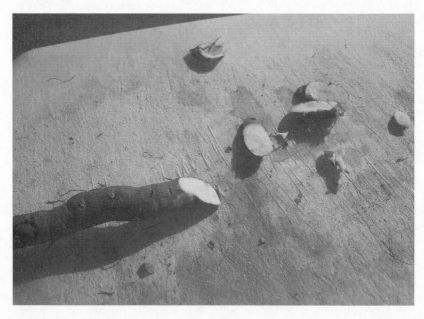

This piece of Japanese knotweed was sliced into little pieces before it dried.

Additionally, be sure to cut the root while it is still fresh. Once it dries out, it becomes very tough and not as easy to cut up —its hard diamond-like exterior is quite possibly the hardest material known to man. Using an electric coffee grinder in an attempt to powder the root does not work. In fact, it did not take long to destroy a brand new grinder with the tough roots —the metal blade simply disappeared. We considered using a sledge hammer, and we might if we find the need to chop up dried Japanese knotweed root in the future, but thought better of it, having no desire to ruin a perfectly good tool. Better just to cut the roots before they dry.

As if the benefits of Japanese knotweed root are not enough, the young stems are edible. We had heard for years about this wonderful plant and had even had the opportunity to sample a bit of it in one of our outdoor skills classes. The spring shoots were harvested and cooked down to an applesauce consistency. A bit of maple syrup was added to sweeten the knotweed mush. Then, the sauce was spooned into pie crust, and we had knotweed pie.

After really starting to focus on the project in the spring, we decided quickly that Japanese knotweed would be on our short list of plants to look for early on. We already knew where to find them.

On our first foraging trip in the spring, we looked for the shoots, but it was still too early. The leaves were just starting to peek out of the ground in the shade of last year's stalks. We cleared some of the dead stalks away. The next week, when we returned, we found some shoots that were the right height, but they were too big around. We wanted shoots no more than our pinky's width. The third week, we found two dozen shoots that were exactly what we were looking to harvest. By the fourth week, the shoots were all too tall and tough to be harvested. The season was very short.

Some of the shoots we ate steamed with a bit of butter, much like asparagus. They have a very mild rhubarb-asparagus flavor. We joke that if rhubarb and asparagus were to have a baby, it would be Japanese knotweed. It offers a wonderful complement for many other foods. Some were also chopped into smaller pieces and baked into a quiche. The rest, which were not consumed fresh from the field, were cleaned, blanched and frozen for use later in the year.

Japanese knotweed is generally considered a weed and very invasive. As is too common, it was probably cultivated as an ornamental that just got away, and with no natural predators, in some places it is starting to squeeze out the natives. Since Japanese knotweed is both edible and medicinal, it just makes sense that we become the predator. As many gardeners discover, fighting with an invasive plant is often just frustrating, but harvesting and using said plant … that is delicious.

Over the years, we have come to understand that many of the plants we have labeled weeds are actually wonderful culinary delights. Aunt Connie, master gardener and a prolific author of books about medicinal and edible plants in the 1970s, recently told us that most gardeners know to eat the weeds. It goes back to being the predator.

We had not thought a lot about it, but one needs to simply look at some of the common names as a clue to their historic uses. Often, when we encounter plants that we cannot or have never identified, I will look to our copy of *Weeds of the Northern US and Canada*.[3] We bought our copy on a whim years ago while wandering around a bookstore. Like too many of our books (and the reason we are wont to purge any of them), it sat unused on the shelf for many years collecting dust. It was rediscovered one day, the dust blown off, and a quick perusal reminded us why we bought it in the first place. It was a wealth of information, not for its intended purpose of helping people control *weeds*, but rather as a way to easily identify them. In addition to lists of common names and great color photos of the plants at various stages of development, it goes into a lot of detail about the structure of the stem, leaves, fruits, flowers, roots, etc.

Using this book, for instance, we found that other common names for burdock, which was introduced from Europe in the 1600s,

First year burdock.

include wild rhubarb, clothbur and beggar's buttons. These names hint at uses as food and crafts, and offer a fairly good description of the plant. I am sure there are more than a few of us who can understand why it might be called clothbur.

Many books reference eating purslane (*Portulaca oleracea*). While the weed book did not list purslane as an edible, it did explain that purslane was introduced from southern Europe in the 1670s. The question was, why would the settlers carry a plant across the ocean for weeks or months in ships with little space to spare for frivolous items? Of course, it must have been brought for a very good reason. Purslane is consumed in Europe, Asia, the Middle East and Mexico. This versatile and delicious edible can be eaten raw in salads, cooked like spinach or added to soups or stews.

Much to our amusement, the reason for concern listed in the weed book is that it is a problem for home gardeners: this tenacious ground cover also hosts certain insects and viral diseases. While such a threat might concern other gardeners, our first thought was,

"What? It's a perennial edible that will save us money on seeds and toil in the garden, and it will probably work as a companion plant for other plants that we might want to grow? How can I get more?!" Interestingly, while the weed book is advising home gardeners about eradicating purslane, online articles state that having it is a sign that the garden soil is healthy, which for us was one more reason to ask it to stay.

We have had purslane growing in our raised garden beds for years. In our ignorance, for many years, we plucked it up by its roots and tossed it into the compost pile. After reading more about the plant, we realize this probably encouraged it to spread throughout our gardens. At some point, we took a less authoritarian role in our garden and started to view the tiny sprouts in a more *wait and see what it is* rather than a *get rid of anything that we did not plant*, as doing so has rewarded us on many occasions.

Such was the case with purslane. We have always thought of it as a volunteer, and for the past couple of years, we have allowed it to grow unchecked except where it might interfere with plants that we are trying to grow. The fact that it was edible was probably not completely lost on us, but until this project we had never taken the opportunity, or time, to try and figure out how to use it. This year, we did eat it.

We enjoyed purslane in salads with some of the other wild food, particularly the greens that nature had freely offered. We added it to stir-fry with foraged roots and hardy garden greens or to fried rice when it was just the purslane, some leftover chicken or pork chops and eggs, and baked it in quiche with some of the many eggs the chickens blessed us with over the summer.

Another *weed* listed in the book that we learned to love this year is common milkweed (*Asclepias syriaca*). We have found that people scorn milkweed because it tends to be prolific in its spread and is often not a welcome addition to lawns. We have welcomed it in our yard for years. At first, it was simply because the flowers are so pleasantly fragrant when in full bloom. Then, one day, our eight-year-old home-schooled daughter rather nonchalantly mentioned that the black and yellow-striped caterpillars crawling all over the milkweed were called *Danaus Plexippus*, and were the larvae of Monarch butterflies. A fevered Internet search and several weeks of observation, which also, happily, illustrated in full color and moving reality the life cycle of an insect, convinced us that this so-called weed deserved an honored place in our landscape.

As if the fact that Monarch butterflies would visit our home if we allowed the milkweed to proliferate was not enough, we discovered lots of other very cool uses for the plant, including learning that the dried dead stems could be used as a source of fiber for making cordage. And, then, there is the additional benefit that milkweed is edible.

Milkweed does present a bit of a quandary for foragers, however. One must decide at which stage it will be picked and eaten, and that decision will depend on what palate-pleasing dish one wishes to consume. All aerial parts of the plant are edible at different stages of development; to propagate, it needs the completely mature seed pods to dry, open and release the seeds for the next generation of plants. Our small patch does not allow much opportunity for experimentation, because we would quickly exhaust our supply. Thankfully, during our travels over the course of the project, we found other much larger colonies of milkweed that allowed us to harvest some during each stage of growth.

The first opportunity comes in the spring, just as everything seems to be awakening, and the tender shoots begin to emerge from the ground. When they are small, less than 8 inches tall, the stems can be cut and eaten. Many books will tell you that they are toxic and must be boiled in several changes of water, but I have eaten them raw immediately after cutting. Sam Thayer discusses this in his excellent book, *The Forager's Harvest*,[4] which we use extensively for plant identification and foraging. The mistake made with regard to milkweed is one of misidentification. Specifically, at some point, someone mistook and mislabeled a look-alike commonly known as dogbane (*Apocynum cannabinum*) as milkweed. Dogbane, which really does not closely resemble milkweed, is poisonous. So pervasive is the rumor, in fact, that many people will insist that the reason Monarch butterflies eat milkweed as their primary food source is that the toxins in the milkweed make them poisonous to potential predators. We have heard the rumor, as well, and even believed it for a time. We may even have shared that untruth, and ignorantly maligned poor milkweed as inedible. Milkweed is not poisonous, and in fact, the fresh young stalks are wonderfully tender, like spring asparagus, and have a very pleasing "green" flavor.

If one can refrain from eating all of the stalks fresh in the spring, one will be rewarded with more opportunities later in the year. Before

The bees enjoy milkweed flowers almost as much as we do.

the flowers open, when they are tiny, little green balls, they are wonderful cooked in a quiche with just a bit of Jerusalem artichoke flour as a thickener. Once they open, they are very sweet. We have read that they can be rendered into sugar, but we did not have any success with doing it. We have sampled them fresh, sucking on the end of the flower stem and nibbling the newly opened flower.

Both the early spring stalks and the flowers make this plant one worth knowing as an edible, but one more part may be used. After the flowers fully mature, they form into pods. The pod was the biggest hit with us, and, as it turns out, it is fairly flexible as a food. The young pods, those up to two inches, can be boiled or steamed and eaten whole. I have read that some people compare them to okra, but in our experience a more apt comparison would be pea pods or green beans. We really enjoyed them served with just a bit of salt and butter.

Very small milkweed pods are delicious when they are boiled and served with a little butter.

When the pods get larger than two inches, they are a little tougher and not generally thought to be good for eating whole. In fact, Sam Thayer does not recommend eating the pods at all. He advises waiting until the pods are between two and four inches, when the silks are starting to form, but before the seeds have turned brown (at which point the whole plant becomes inedible until next year), and harvesting the pods for the silks. He boils the silks into a faux cheese.

Cheese is a much beloved and delighted food in our house, and we enjoy all sorts of cheeses. We have made some of our own, and cheese-making is one of those projects we intend to do more often. Cheese lends itself well to being stuffed into things like pasta shells, and so, when we read this tidbit from Mr. Thayer, the idea of making a sort of stuffed shell from the milkweed pods took hold and would not let go.

The result was what we started calling milkweed pod lasagna. We opened the pods, removing the silks, which we boiled per Sam Thayer's instructions. Then, we mixed the silks with egg and more

Milkweed pod lasagna … delicious!

cheese to make a lasagna-like filling. The pod hulls were boiled in salt water until they were just tender. The filling was stuffed into the shells. A tomato-based meat sauce was spooned over the stuffed shells, topped with grated cheese and baked until the cheese was melted and slightly browned. It was delightfully yummy.

We made the lasagna a couple of times over the summer, and it was everything we had hoped it would be when we were first struck with the idea to make it. These stuffed morsels are a fantastic replacement for pasta shells. We even served our milkweed lasagna at our summer party, and it was a hit with the guests who were brave enough to try it.

One day, while cruising around on the Internet, we found a Canadian company that sold preserved foraged food products, like wild blackberry jam or pickled fiddleheads, both of which are common fare. The one product that most interested us, however, was the pickled milkweed pods, and we figured if they could do it, we could too. So, using some of the milkweed pods a friend had brought us

Pickled pods.

and a standard cucumber pickling recipe, we pickled a few jars of the milkweed pods.

If we had to describe the taste, we would say it was peppery, like a pepperoncini, but not hot. The pods we used were perhaps a little too old, as they were a bit stringy, but they were very tasty, and after struggling for years to find a suitable place on our quarter acre for growing pickling cukes, and failing that, buying them in bulk from local farmers, we have decided that a better way to go is to harvest milkweed pods, which are free, and pickle those instead. Interestingly, finding that website also made us realize that many of the foods we foraged this year are actually gourmet treats.

In the world of wild foraging, things change fast, and if nothing else taught us that lesson over the course of our project, it was the shoots. One day they would be perfect for harvesting, and almost the next day, too big. The truth of the phrase *grows like weeds* was painfully evident as we missed out on a second or third (small) harvest of some of the shoots we had enjoyed. Luckily for us, we were given a second chance with roots, being able to harvest them in both spring and summer — if we know what to look for.

CHAPTER 4

Berries

W HILE SPRING AND EARLY SUMMER ARE PRIME TIME for gathering roots, shoots and greens, by mid-summer, Mother Nature
starts dressing things up a bit, and adding some color and sweet flavor. We anxiously await the end of June, because that is when the
berries start to ripen.

The warm sun gently prods them into ripeness, and biting into
the tender flesh of a berry freshly plucked from its stalk produces a
delightful burst of sweetness. Eating berries fresh and raw is a trea-
sured time for our family, when we gorge ourselves on all that we can
find. As seasonal eaters, we take our fill of whatever we have growing, and then, if any is left over, we store it. Whether in the form of
jellies or jams, frozen or dried, they serve as a reminder of summer
throughout the year. When it comes to foraging, berries are the no-
brainer of foods, because almost everyone can recognize at least one
type of berry and many will pick berries without even considering
that they are foraging.

While early foraged food can certainly be stored for later, berries really are the first opportunity for any substantial food storage.
Greens are short-lived and best eaten fresh in salads and soups,

although they can be dried and stored. Roots must be picked before the plant starts growing again in earnest. Otherwise, they can become tough and woody. Likewise, the window for picking tender young shoots is small. The berry season (allowing for the fact that there are several varieties that grow in succession with overlapping seasons), in general, is pretty long, and berries lend themselves well to a variety of storage options.

Strawberries herald in the berry season for us. We have tried over the years to grow our own, but not with a lot of success. Our tiny patch provides just a trickle of berries, one here, one there, but never enough for more than a taste, and certainly not enough to store any for later.

Strawberry plants are fairly resilient and grow back year after year with little assistance. The parent plants send out their daughter runners, and the patch gets a little bigger, until we unwittingly trample it, or run it over with the mower. It is a tiny and unreliable food source, and if we had to depend on these, we would go hungry. Still, we like strawberries, and so we support our local growers by picking very large (and expensive) quantities of strawberries every year. A quarter of our sixty-pound haul is usually eaten on the way home from the field. After we have polished off another quarter eating strawberry shortcake for a week, the rest end up as jam for the winter. We have not found very many wild strawberries, and those we have found were tiny, and not terribly prolific. Fortunately, nature has seen fit to provide us with a whole host of other options to help satisfy our needs.

Behind our house, a trail winds through the small patch of woods and meanders in a horseshoe to the field where we focused our foraging efforts this year. Halfway between the trail's entrance and our house, a smaller, narrower trail turns off to the right. It leads through a small clearing, goes back into the woods and stops at a brook. The clearing is chock full of low-bush blueberries (*Vaccinium angustifolium*) and their companions, sheep laurel and wintergreen.

We discovered the blueberry field many years ago and have wandered back there, occasionally, during the summer months to check out how well the blueberries were growing. We have come to know its character, which can be quite stingy at times with its fruits. A few years ago, we had a banner harvest, gathering two gallons of pea-sized blueberries from the field, most of which ended up frozen. Unfortunately, the last few years in this spot have been pretty desolate from a harvesting perspective, and the berries we do manage to harvest are tiny.

The wooded area is mostly new-growth forest, predominately populated by fast-growing softwoods, like white pine (*Pinus strobus*). What there is of an understory is mostly low-bush blueberry plants. The kinds of foliage that proliferate in the area and some other clues, like the rusty pieces of barbed wire fencing, lead us to believe that the area was once razed, probably for farm land. From what we have read, when an area that was previously cultivated is abandoned back to nature, first the grasses move in, then the low woody bushes (like blueberry), then softwood trees and then the hardwoods.

In addition to the field of blueberry bushes, dotted all along the trail are smaller stands. This year, as the seasons progressed, we watched the field and the bushes along the path leading to it, saw the bushes flower and paid attention to when the flowers died back, giving way to the fruit. We noted the little green berries growing and believed we would have another banner blueberry year. Finally, they ripened to perfect little blue spheres, and on the Fourth of July weekend, we decided it was time to take advantage of the bounty.

We are fairly certain that at times our girls wish they had normal parents, the kind for whom the word "fun" is manifest as a visit to an amusement park (and at least four are within a short drive of our house) or a day spent languishing on the beach (a couple of miles away), and not to say that those things are not *fun*, but those are not the sorts of activities that we typically enjoy doing. Vacation, for us, often means an opportunity for activities we do not always make time or have time for in our day-to-day lives, like picking blueberries.

Although our intent was to pick berries, the best part was not bringing home three pounds of free food. The best part was listening to our girls, who never complained, not once, not even when they were sweating or being bitten by the hordes of hungry mosquitoes, in spite of the dull aches from bending over to pick from the low bushes. Instead, they chatted, about the noise they heard in the woods, about the dog who was complaining, as only our impatient and anxiety-ridden beagle can do ... and about the picking.

"Did you notice that every time there's a clump of four blueberries, one of them is green?"

"Yeah! It is!"

And they talked about eating blueberries, and blueberry cobbler and blueberry pancakes and all of the wonderful foods we could have once we got home with all of those blueberries. We did not spend the holiday standing in lines at a local amusement park or burning on the beach, but it was a fun day — one that our girls will remember fondly in December, when they are spooning into their mouths each morsel of blueberry pancake and savoring each bite as the sweet juice of our summer haul bursts with the memory of that day in the woods, picking blueberries and listening to the dog whine, because he wanted to go home and take a nap.

We filled all five of the pint jars we had brought with us, and probably had another jar's worth besides that ended up in our bellies. The berries that did make it back to the house were loaded into the newly built solar dehydrator, constructed using bits and pieces of the flotsam and jetsam we always seem to collect in our yard. When they were sufficiently shriveled, we put them into a single pint jar and stored them in the kitchen cabinet. Since then, these wrinkly, little morsels have been added to yogurt, oatmeal, home-made trail mixes, breads and pancakes, and they have even been eaten, out of hand, like raisins.

If this had been our only outing for blueberries, we would have considered ourselves fortunate and been thankful for what we had

Five pints of blueberries was a great harvest.

been given. But, life has a funny way of rewarding those who are truly grateful for the good things in their lives. We had no idea that we would be the recipients of this type of blessing.

Maine is known for a number of things like lobster, sandy beaches and blueberries. This last is because wild blueberries grow abundantly throughout the state. The Wyman family, which owns a nationally recognized brand of frozen berries, did not create the blueberry barrens that have proven so profitable for their family, but someone in their ancestry had the foresight to begin harvesting and marketing the "wild" (low-bush as opposed to high-bush) berries.

We have been told that, as recently as fifty years ago, before many houses were constructed here, people often came to our neighborhood in search of wild blueberries, which were, apparently, all over the place. Unfortunately, residential and commercial development has severely reduced the number of bushes, but they do still thrive, usually unnoticed, in the underbrush and in areas where people just do not look.

It is not just our neighborhood, however, where the berries like to grow. While the heavily developed southern Maine is no longer renowned for its wild stashes of berries, there are still plenty to be found for those who care to look. In a neighboring town, Eric works in a relatively new industrial park that was carved out of the forest that filled the entire area not too many years ago. As we discovered, quite by accident, this land once supported a vast number of both high-bush and low-bush blueberries, many of which are still there.

The realization began innocently enough one day while at work. The company had purchased the building beside their parking lot, and cleared and paved a pathway to connect the two buildings for forklift trucks and foot traffic. This particular day was warm and pleasant. On an errand to the new building, I was walking along with one of my co-workers. We crossed through the small forested border between the two pieces of property, and I spied a small, three-foot-tall high-bush blueberry (*Vaccinium corymbosum*) sparsely covered with clumps of ripe berries.

"Look! Blueberries!" I pointed out to my co-worker, and we continued on our way.

My plan was to return later for a snack. It was just one small lone bush, with only a few berries — not enough to store, but plenty for a nutrient-packed nibble. Sometime later in the day, my co-worker informed me that someone else had eaten all of, what I had thought to be, my snack. It was disappointing, but I figured, first come, first served.

Much later in the day, on another errand to the building, I thought I would just look, and to my surprise, I noted that the blueberries were still there, in the same numbers as before. This time, I did not hesitate. I picked one of the berries and popped it into my mouth. Ah! The sweet, juicy berry erupted in a torrent of flavor over my tongue. The much smaller low-bush berries we had picked were sweet but not terribly juicy.

As I enjoyed a few of the berries, I never considered that the blueberry bush might have cousins living nearby. I made the same mistake as my co-worker, who failed to see the bush, even after I had pointed it out to him. I was not seeing, and even without looking, I just assumed that the one blueberry bush I had harvested for my late afternoon snack was the only one in the area.

I know better. Even with the huge field near our house that is, quite literally, carpeted with low-bush blueberries, there are still other plants growing all along the trail and back between the trees where the sunlight dapples through the canopy. Blueberries do not grow in isolation. My only defense for my blind short-sightedness is that I was at work and focused on what I had to do for the company.

A few days later, by some odd quirk of fate, I needed a ride home from work, and the plan was for Wendy to pick me up. Because of a scheduling conflict, when my workday ended, she was not able to be there right away, and so I decided to start walking, planning to meet her somewhere between work and home.

Starting out, I passed by the bush that had provided my earlier snack. Berries in hand, I headed down the road. I scanned the area while walking to see what plants and animals I could identify by sight or sound, a fun game that also helps to hone awareness building.

I had barely walked a quarter of a mile, when I noticed through the dabbled sunlight what had to be a six-foot-tall high-bush blueberry plant loaded with clumps of berries. It was growing along the border of the property where the line of trees had been left to provide a type of natural fence. I picked two large handfuls of berries, noting the spot so that I could return with Wendy, and containers, to pick more. These berries, too, were explosively delicious.

I continued my stroll munching, berries as my mind wandered in awe at the incredible gift I had just been given. This bush, and a couple of others nearby, were all happily, and productively, growing on the property lines. More importantly, no one seemed to have any idea that they were there, and so they went unnoticed and unpicked.

Shortly beyond these bushes, I turned onto another road toward home. This road had some residential homes, a public works building, two schools, a baseball field and a few commercial buildings in a stretch that is a mile or so long. Continuing against traffic, and encouraged by finding more bushes, I began peering closely into the shade looking for others along the next mile before the road opened into a crowded residential neighborhood.

I noted dozens more bushes, some as tall as twelve feet, and all of them bursting with bright blue clumps of berries that could be seen from the road, some ten to twenty feet away. By this time, I was terribly excited and could not wait to share my find.

Indeed, fortune shined on me that day in more ways than one. My mother happened to pass me as I was walking along the road, and she gave me a ride the rest of the way. At home, I grabbed Wendy and some buckets, and we hopped in the car and hurried back to the industrial park. Once there, I instructed her to start looking on the sides of the road, and as she gazed out of the window looking for the blueberries, the phrase we coined, *high-speed foraging*, was born. We drove along at the speed limit looking for the bushes I had found earlier. I am not certain that she believed how big, or full, the bushes were. I am pretty certain she did not believe that we would be able to see them from the road at twenty-five miles per hour. But, when she spied her first clump from the passenger window, she told me to stop. I quickly pulled over, and we grabbed our bins, jumped the ditch and commenced picking the huge berries.

Sometimes wild foraging can be a bit discomfiting, especially where there is car traffic, and one knows one is completely visible. There is always that concern that someone might not like having people picking whatever they're picking, and while it was pretty obvious that no one wanted those berries, the trees looked to be at the end of a residential driveway. We decided not to spend too much time at the first tree, hopped back in the car and found more bushes, equally full, but in front of businesses rather than homes. After a half hour in a kind of hit-and-run pattern of picking and moving on, we ended up with four pints, almost as many berries as had taken us two hours at the blueberry barrens on July 4.

We returned twice over the next couple of weeks, and in addition to picking from the dozens of high-bush plants, we also found several places with low-bush blueberries. We harvested a bit from both. During the season, which lasted for nearly a month from the ripening of the low-bushes to the final berries picked from the high-bushes, we harvested just over seven pounds of blueberries. If we had found the high-bush plants earlier in the season, or if we could have picked more between first finding them and the point when we realized they were too ripe, we would certainly have had a much larger haul. We decided to dehydrate the high-bush blueberries and add them to our dried berry stash.

In our yard, we have a lovely little blueberry bush that we planted and some wild blueberries that just grow there. None of those bushes ever seem quite as productive as their wild counterparts. The lesson we are learning is that so many of the foods that we want in our diet are readily available, for free, and we usually have better luck finding them in the wild than we do cultivating them on our small property.

Of course, before we became fully aware of that lesson, we had already invested in all of these wonderful plants. One cultivated plant that has been a great producer, but that also has a wild cousin, is our black raspberry (*Rubus occidentalis*) bramble. Whether it is just a great plant or this one time we found the exact right mix of what the plant loves best to flourish, the brambles seem to be very happy growing against the neighbor's fence on the southeast side of our property, and they grow prolifically. Each year, we have more than

Blueberries: A Maine treasure.

enough raspberries to munch, while leaving sufficient numbers to put in the freezer for the long cold winter.

The brambles are so happy with their location, in fact, that they try to spread all over the place, including over the fence and into the neighbor's yard. Luckily, he does not mind the crazy, thorn-covered stalks growing everywhere, and we are careful to prune both sides of the fence … and to share the berries with him and his wife when we are harvesting. In spite of our amateurish pruning, we manage to gather berries every year. One year, we made the mistake of cutting them back to four inches high (the instruction was supposed to be four *feet* above the ground, but was given in haste and the wrong measurement was spoken — Oops!), and they still grew back, just as aggressively as before, and provided us with a bumper crop of sweet, juicy fruits.

Berry canes grow wild all over the place and are more than generous with their fruit.

Not to be out done, Mother Nature rose to the challenge, and gifted us with a not insignificant number of red raspberry (*Rubus idaeus*) brambles growing wild against the side of our house. These wild berries ripen at about the same time as our cultivated ones, and our granddaughter loves nothing more than to graze the berry brambles. As yet, the wild brambles do not produce much beyond what our granddaughter picks, but who knows what the next season will be like.

Blackberries are forager-friendly plants that many people recognize and will pick when the berries are fully ripe. There are no poisonous look-alikes. Like other people who recognize and pick the ripe berries, over the years we have made a point of picking blackberries whenever we find them.

A few years ago, while walking along a trail near our house, we noticed a large number of blackberry brambles that were holding large clusters of ripe berries. We were carrying very little gear — a backpack and some water bottles — but as luck would have it, that backpack contained some pieces of paper, which we quickly folded into containers to hold the blackberries. We worked our way in from the clear path toward the center of the tangled thorny stems, and after about thirty minutes, carefully worked our way back out, like unwinding a Maypole. We snacked all the way home, and only a few, if any, of the berries actually made it into our house. We talk about going back there to pick berries, but for whatever reason never make it.

When we started this project, the intent was to pick berries along that trail, but as the season wore on, we decided to concentrate our efforts on foraging closer to home. On the edges of the field near our house, we found many brambles. At first, we were not sure if they were blackberry or raspberry, but as the season progressed, we noticed some distinct differences between the flowers on the brambles growing in our yard, which we know are raspberry, and the brambles in the field. We knew these were blackberries, and the discovery of a novel berry, i.e., one that we had not tried (and failed) to cultivate in our yard, was incredibly exciting (although we would not have turned up our noses at another source of (free) raspberries).

Near the end of July, we started picking blackberries in the field. The berries were small, and the brambles did not seem to have produced much. It could be that they were competing too much for the few nutrients in the sandy soil of the hill on which they were growing. It could be that the brambles were still young, and that in the future, they will grow stronger and produce more. It could be that the brambles were incredibly prolific, but that the wild turkeys or other wild life that inhabit the area (or the people who live right next to the field) beat us to the harvest.

We managed a meager one pint harvest of berries, and since we were still pretty full of raspberries, we decided to store these in the freezer. Some plants still had not-quite-ripe berries, which we figured we could probably go back for later, and if that field still did not yield much, we mused, we could always check out the trail where we had found blackberries before.

As the summer was preparing for its great finale and the time for our party was growing nearer, we started looking for the plants we wanted to serve. Having tried milkweed pods in several different dishes, we wanted to include a lasagna we had made using the pods. The pods on the few plants in our yard were too large to be eaten, but we had noted that the plants closer to the coast seemed to ripen later. So we headed over to Indian Jane Rock to the field where we knew milkweed grew.

Some people do not believe in luck. It is fate. Some people believe there is no such thing as either, and that fortune is simply a matter of the choices one makes. Whatever one's personal beliefs, we have come to not question when given what can only be viewed as a magnificent gift.

Right there, alongside the trail we had walked on so very many occasions stood the biggest cluster of blackberry brambles we had ever seen. Some stood tall enough to dwarf us, and it was clear that no one was harvesting the berries, because a few had ripened beyond peak to the mushy stage where picking them equates to a handful of blackberry pulp. On the day of discovery, we only picked a pound of berries.

A few days later, armed with six quart-sized cardboard containers (the kind we take to the pick-your-own strawberry fields), we returned. With rain threatening, we had debated not going, but realized that if we did not make this trip, we might not make it back before the rest of the berries rotted unpicked. In just over a half hour, the five of us filled five of the six containers (and ate quite a few of the berries, to keep our strength up while we picked, right?) before the rain came and sent us running for cover. Each quart container of berries weighed five pounds, and we had barely made a dent in the patch.

While unsure we would still find any usable berries, we decided, a week later, to head back over to Indian Jane Rock for more berries, which we planned to serve at our summer party. There were still plenty of berries to pick, but we noted that the deer had made paths into the center of the tangle and bedded down, nibbling on the lower hanging berries. The stand of brambles was flattened and trampled in several places, and while the deer paths made convenient points of entry for us to work, it was a little disheartening to see all of the ruined berries and damaged canes.

We filled seven more quart containers on the last trip. Some of these berries found their way into fresh, delicious pastries and cobblers. There is little that is more satisfying than eating food made with fresh berries picked only days, and sometimes hours, before. Most of the twelve and a half of pounds of blackberries were frozen to be enjoyed over the winter.

The real benefit of freezing berries is that it gives us options. They can be made into smoothies, slightly thawed, spooned over shortcakes and topped with whipped cream, stirred into yogurt or made into jam. If we have picked more than can be comfortably eaten before next season, the excess can be made into what we affectionately refer to as *freezer-berry wine*, which simply comprises all of the berries left in the freezer at the beginning of summer.

Strawberries, blackberries, raspberries and blueberries are much loved and easy to identify. While the average person may not be able to identify the plant on which any of those four grow, most could identify the berries, even in the wild.

One of the berries we have most wanted to try for years, and which we resolved to include in our project, is a berry that does not even really look like one to most people. It actually looks like a flower on a shrub that can grow as tall as thirty-two feet high. The shrub, staghorn sumac (*Rhus typhina*), grows all over the state of Maine. When we traveled through New York into Pennsylvania, we noticed staghorn sumac growing all along the sides of the road in those states as well.

It gets its common name, staghorn, because the bark is fuzzy like the horn of a stag, and each summer, a bright red berry cluster that resembles a candle flame forms at the end of each branch. Another common name for the berries is lemonade berries, and in survival food circles, it is used as *survival lemonade*. It is one of those plants we heard about for years, and always intended to try, but we just could not seem to get to the flowers when they were ripe, being too distracted by other things in life. If picked too early or too late, they will not have the desired flavor. In addition, even though we had always wanted to try it, we had no knowledge of how to store the plant for later, and so harvesting was never as much of a priority for us.

As luck would have it, a conversation with a friend resulted in the gift of a grocery bag full of the fruits, and we served sumac lemonade to the guests who wished to try it at our summer party. After reading different methods for making the drink, we chose the simplest one: steep the berries in cold water for fifteen minutes, strain liquid through cheesecloth, add sugar if desired and serve. The most amazing part of the whole experience was that, fully ripe and properly prepared, sumac lemonade tastes just like lemonade — no lemons necessary. Given that, as locavores, citrus is not often on our menu, it was quite a treat to find a tangy beverage as a substitute for the beloved summer beverage. We will very likely go out of our way to find staghorn sumac in the future.

While intentional foraging was our plan, there were some occasions when we engaged in opportunistic foraging. The blueberries in the industrial park might fall into the opportunistic category, although when we returned with buckets in hand, it transformed into intentional. Foraging rose hips was all opportunistic.

Rose hips are another one of those plants that we had always planned to take advantage of and just never had. Fortunately for us, *Rosa rugosa*, or beach roses, are widely popular in our area as an ornamental plant and a hedgerow. It also seems to grow commonly enough near the edges of the roads. A few grow down the road near our stop sign, although the plants do not get enough sun or nutrients, and so they are small and do not produce much of a crop of the coveted rose hips. For years, we have seen the rose hips each fall and resolve to pick a few, but a lack of knowledge about how to prepare them has always stayed our hand.

After some cursory research about uses for rose hips and the easiest preservation methods, we decided to harvest them to make tea. Unlike most of our other foraging expeditions, we never set aside time for the specific purpose of harvesting rose hips. Instead, when we were visiting local establishments, where rose hips were part of the landscape, we took the opportunity to pick a few.

In the grassy strip that divides the public sidewalk from the parking lot of a very small local shopping center where there is a pizza joint, a UPS store and one of those second-hand designer clothes shops grows a very beautiful hedge of *Rosa rugosa*. One day, when we were running an errand there, the rose hips just seemed to call, and so we picked around two pints.

At our local supermarket, the strips between parking areas have also been landscaped with *Rosa rugosa*. After shopping on a few occasions during the summer, when the rose hips were fully ripe, we stopped not to smell the flowers, but to pick the fruits.

Rose hips are a member of the apple family, and indeed the ripe, raw rose hip tastes mildly of apple. While we have seen dozens of recipes for using them, we opted to dry them for use as a stand-alone tea, or as part of a blend.

Out of curiosity, one day while in the grocery store, we decided to see how much rose hips cost. In the organic tea aisle, we found several blends of tea that included rose hips, at a cost of $5 or more for a box of twenty tea bags. Spending ten minutes gathering the rose hips after our weekly shopping certainly seemed worthwhile when we considered how much money we potentially saved by foraging.

Of all our foraged foods, berries were probably our favorite. Certainly they are our girls' favorite. Berries are easily identified, are palate-pleasing even for picky eaters, are easy to pick and are full of wonderful vitamins and minerals. While we are very interested in expanding our knowledge of wild plants, if the only one we really knew were berries, we would still consider ourselves fortunate.

CHAPTER 5

Gifts from the Trees

WHEN FIRST LOOKING FOR A HOUSE TO BUY, we had some very specific wants in mind. We wanted at least an acre of land with a yard large enough for our dog, our children and our hoped-for gardens. We wanted a nice-sized kitchen with lots of cabinet space. We wanted lots of storage and would have liked a basement or garage. What we got was nothing that we had planned for. The lot is tiny, there is no storage, and the kitchen is, basically, a galley kitchen with no drawers (a fact that did not fully occur to us until after we had closed the deal). At first we fixated on what we did not have and failed to see the bounty surrounding us. It took a while, but we have (finally) come to really appreciate the exact location of our home. For every one of the features our home lacks, there are several natural elements in our surrounding area that make this place perfect for us.

We are discovering how fortunate we are to live where there is a large diversity of not only flora and fauna, but ecosystems. To the east a few miles, the Atlantic Ocean laps both rocky coast line and sandy beaches, each with its own unique blend of forage options including seaweeds and shellfish. To the north a few miles, there is a large salt marsh that supports a vast number of birds, fish and plants. A few miles west, the rolling grasslands have served as farms for years. Further west, the hills grow into the foothills of the White Mountains of New Hampshire and the Appalachian Mountains. A bit south, there is a good-sized river running from the mountains to the sea, supplying water to the surrounding towns and supporting a menagerie of aquatic wildlife.

Throughout all of the varying terrains are trees. In fact much of Maine is heavily wooded. When we first drove into the state, after driving from the southwest where we had been living for nearly two years, the first thing that struck me was the smell. It was clean and fresh … and pine. The next was that there were a lot of trees, and it was unlike any coastal community I had ever seen. Most of the time, near the coast, one can tell when the beach is near because the terrain tends to flatten out, the trees grow more sparse, and the sky seems to open up. Not so in Maine. Many times we were actually on the beach before we knew we were so close to the ocean. The trees are tall and thick, and everywhere.

Even on our tiny quarter acre, we have several species of trees. While the lot seemed barren when we first bought it — an empty slate for us to fill — the fact is that there were trees. In the front, we had a couple of small stands of swamp maple and some oak saplings. In the back, we have black cherry (*Prunus serotina*) and, behind the fence, on the hill that dips down into the brook, more swamp maples, a couple of poplars and more black cherry. The large swath of land (probably equivalent to our entire lot size) that contains the brook dividing our property from our neighbors is heavily wooded and mostly shaded all summer long. Down the road — less than a tenth of a mile — is a twenty-five-acre undeveloped heavily wooded area (mostly evergreens).

Given the area where we live, it was natural that when we first started active plant identification we began with trees. It was an easy choice because they are always there spring, summer, fall and winter, and in our area, they are everywhere we look.

As we will say repeatedly, one of the first things we did when we started learning tree identification was to find a book. For our area, one of the best we found is a primer published by the State of Maine Forestry Department, *The Forest Trees of Maine*,[1] which is freely available as a download from their website (but a print copy can also be purchased — we have both). It contains both summer and winter identification keys. The summer key focuses on leaf formations, while the winter key focuses on bark and branch formations. Cross-referencing both keys was most helpful for positively identifying the trees, as we needed to see the leaves to be sure that we had the right tree. Even then, we were not always 100 percent sure or correct.

Indigenous people in this area knew the trees very well. They used them for food and medicine, tools and dishes, crafts, shelter and fuel. To them, the trees have a spirit and a purpose, like all life they encountered, and the gifts of the trees were highly valued.

Over time, we have developed a greater appreciation of the trees and their gifts, but we had no idea the breadth of knowledge the trees had to share with anyone willing to listen. In the beginning, we never imagined that trees had more to give than just the materials we took from them. We have discovered that trees provide a wealth of information about the weather, the coming growing seasons and the population density of the animals that rely on them for food. Even with all that we have gleaned from our brothers, the trees, we know that there is still much more to learn. The first lesson is that of being gracious and thankful recipients of their gifts, which the trees willingly offer — in abundance.

We first began to listen to the trees when we decided to learn how to tap our maple trees. They are one of the first deciduous trees to wake up at the end of winter, and we eagerly await their signs that spring is well on its way. The first is the tiny little buds and the reddening of the stems of the red maples (*Acer rubrum*). When the tips of the stems start getting red, it is our sign that it is time to harvest the first of the gifts from the trees for the year, the gift of maple syrup.

We have been tapping our maples for five seasons. The first year, we went to the hardware store and on a fluke, bought a couple of taps, a drill bit and some buckets — just to try it out. Why not, we reasoned. We had the trees. We used plastic bags from the grocery store to cover the buckets and keep debris out of our sap. We boiled the sap in a kettle using a borrowed turkey fryer. Our three maple trees gave us just under a gallon of maple syrup, and when our neighbors saw that we had tapped our trees, they said we could also tap theirs if we wanted to.

When we first started in 2008, we knew very little. Most of what we thought we knew, we had learned from visiting commercial sugar houses and reading books and online articles. As has been wisely observed, experience is the best teacher, and much of what we thought we knew was disproved with the doing.

Conventional wisdom dictates that the sugaring season starts around the end of February and lasts until the end of March (and if we are lucky, the sap will run into April). In Maine, the last Sunday of March is traditionally Maple Syrup Sunday, and many area farms will host a pancake breakfast to mark the end of the season. Books will also talk about the kinds of maples that can be tapped and how to boil the sap down. Both of those pieces of advice are geared toward commercial sugar houses, however, and a home sugarer, whose goal is syrup for the family, will take the same stance as a home canner, which is to say that what is good for the big guys is often unnecessary for the home producer.

What we learned first was that all maple trees can be tapped. The first time we tapped a maple tree, we did not realize there were other types, or at least it did not occur to us that we should be worried about whether our maple was a swamp maple, a silver maple (*Acer saccharinum*) or a sugar maple (*Acer saccharum*). It was a maple tree, and in our ignorance, we just assumed that any maple tree will produce sap that can, then, be turned into syrup. Our assumption was absolutely correct. We do not have any sugar maples on our property, but we did have maple trees, and so we used what we had and made syrup.

We have learned since that first experiment with making syrup that the sugar content in the sap may vary from one type of tree to another. The sap in a sugar maple has the highest sugar content, but as we discovered, the boiled sap from a maple tree — any maple tree — makes maple syrup.

Our education in syrup making continues to expand. At the Mother Earth News Fair in 2012, we were fortunate to meet an amazing gentleman named Craig Russell, the president of the Society for the Preservation of Poultry Antiquities. As an old-time homesteader, he told us some interesting facts about trees and their syrup-making abilities. We were informed that many trees, not usually tapped for their sap, will produce an amazing syrup. In particular, he mentioned that nut trees can also be tapped. We had no idea.

Birch trees can also be tapped for their sap, although one needs more birch sap to make a sweet syrup than amount of sap needed to make maple syrup as the sugar content in birch sap is much lower. Twice as much birch sap is needed to make one gallon of syrup as compared to the sap to syrup ratio for maple syrup, which explains why maple syrup is a much more popular treat.

Some trees cannot be tapped, however. For instance, oak trees do not provide sap the way maple trees do. We would prefer not to reveal how we discovered this secret of the trees, but suffice it to say that it is no longer a secret for us ... and ignore that little hole in the oak tree by the road.

Humorous and ironic mistakes aside, we have started to develop a kind of sixth sense of when the trees should be tapped. Initially, we depended on the calendar to tell us when to tap the trees, but we have found that watching for signs, like the temperature (above freezing during the day followed by below freezing a night) and the emerging leaf buds, tells us a lot more about whether the sap is running than a bunch of numbers on a piece of paper.

We have found that, if we depended solely on the calendar, we would have missed a couple of seasons over the past few years. Some years are very long with good sap flow, and we become inundated with sap and overwhelmed with trying to keep up. Other years, the season is very short and/or starts much earlier than is expected. The winter of 2011-2012 was very short and very mild, and by the middle of January, we started noticing signs that it was time to tap. On January 28, 2012, a good three weeks or so before one would tap according to the calendar, we put in our first taps. By the first week in March, the season was over, and on Maine Maple Sunday, the taps had been pulled, cleaned and stored, and the last jar of syrup had long since been boiled and sealed.

Between our trees and our neighbors' trees, we are currently tapping fifteen trees each year. When we decided to really make sugaring a part of our homesteading, we invested in metal buckets and taps. As the buckets fill, we pour them into a central collecting barrel. We paid $20 for a repurposed food-grade barrel from a local vendor, who collects them from area restaurants. We bought three, two of which are used for rainwater collection and the last one is used only during sugaring season, to hold our sap until we have time to boil it.

Boiling, the longest part of the process, transforms approximately forty gallons of sap into a single gallon of delicious amber syrup. Unfortunately, activities, such as a full-time job, compete for our extra time, and there are weeks when we are able to boil the sap only on the weekend. The barrel works well at the beginning of the season because the temperatures are low enough at night to keep the sap from spoiling. Toward the end of the season, the barrel provides a clear indication that the days of collecting are nearing the end, as the sap tends to get cloudy when the weather does not allow it sufficient cooling. In the early years, we were not sure about boiling the cloudy sap for syrup, but through some trial and error, we discovered that the cloudy sap was fine for our personal syrup production.

Our set-up for boiling the sap is rudimentary, at best, especially compared to commercial production. The first year, we used a turkey fryer, but as we started harvesting more sap, we needed something bigger and that would use a more readily available fuel. We now boil the sap over an open fire in a cinder-block fire pit we build every spring. We have two aluminum roasting pans measuring 20-by-22-by-6 inches that can each hold eleven gallons of sap. They are suspended over the open fire, which is fueled by standing dry wood foraged from the local area. Using the two pans, we can boil forty gallons of sap (which yields about a gallon of syrup) in roughly five hours of continuous boiling. This takes a lot of work, because the sap needs to be kept boiling through the whole process, which means the fire has to be continually fed.

We boil the sap outside down to about an inch of liquid left in the roasting pans, and then we pour it through a felt filter into a kettle, which we bring into the house and finish boiling on the electric stovetop. When it reaches a temperature of 7° above the boiling point of water, it is syrup. Or, we wait until it bubbles up the sides of the pan, add five minutes, and call it done. The hot syrup is poured into clean and sterile canning jars, topped with a new canning lid, and hot-water bathed for ten minutes to ensure the jars are sealed. We store it with the rest of our canned goods, and refrigerate the jars when we open them.

The initial investment, including our taps, buckets with lids, storage barrel and pans (the only part that would not necessarily need to be purchased), was pretty expensive, but compared to purchasing pure maple syrup, we figure we make out pretty good. Even in a bad year, where we might gather and store only three gallons of syrup for our personal use (which is to say not including the quarts we give to our neighbors in payment for allowing us to use their trees), we estimate a savings of $240 if we were to purchase an equal amount of syrup at the grocery store.

If syrup were the only food we were able to gather by tapping the maples, we would be satisfied, but we have made other consumables using the sap. We successfully brewed what we called maple beer using unfinished, concentrated sap.

The boiling process required to make syrup simply drives off the excess water, leaving behind a more concentrated sugary water. As any brewer can attest, turning juices or sugar water into alcohol is a simple process of allowing yeast (either wild caught, as described in the wonderful work *Wild Fermentation* by Sandor Katz,[2] or in commercial form) to eat the sugars. The concentration of sugar determines the final alcohol content of your brew.[3] In short, sugary, raw juice, left open and unrefrigerated on a counter will, eventually, become wine (and, then, vinegar, if left open).

We applied that same principle when making our maple brew. We boiled to concentrate the sugar content, and when it reached a level that would give us a brew that would be 5 percent alcohol by volume (ABV), we cooled the liquid and added a brewing yeast. We put the sap into a container with an airlock to allow the fermentation process to take place. The sum total of the ingredients were just that — sap from the maple tree and a package of yeast. A typical beer is fermented for about three weeks and then bottled. We watched the airlock, and when the bubbles stopped forming, the brew was ready.

There is no way to accurately describe the taste, because it did not taste anything like the commercial beers available on the market, and neither was it like any of the beer kits available for home brewing projects. There were no hops for bittering the brew, and it was not sweet, like syrup, because the yeast had consumed most of the sugar. It had a very pleasant mild flavor. The closest we can come to describing the taste is to say it was "crisp and clean" with a hint of alcohol.

We are very fortunate to live in an area with many trees, and while we depend heavily on the maple tree for syrup, a unique brew and other non-food items, it is not the only one that is very generous with its gifts.

On the opposite end of the growing season from spring sugaring is the apple harvest, which occurs in the fall. Most people are able to recognize apples in the trees, if they find them. For those with a bit more experience with apple trees, recognizing them before the apples form when there are just flowers, can be a real treat.

Here in Maine, apple trees proliferate. Until only a few decades ago, the state was heavily involved in agriculture and farming, and as recently as the 1980s, there were still large farms all over southern Maine. It was fairly common practice when establishing a farm to plant fruit trees, which in our climate meant apple trees, to help feed the large families which rarely had extra cash. They were a perfect addition to a self-sufficient homestead. An average apple tree can produce over 800 pounds of fruit per year. For home use, the apples do not need to be perfect to be canned and stored as applesauce, made into a pie or simply eaten whole as a snack. Numerous varieties can be stored in a cold cellar for many months, which makes them quite a treat in parts of the country where very little is growing for long periods of time.

Unfortunately, as the farming generations grow older and pass away, these large farms are being subdivided into suburban house lots. As the land is divided and sold and redeveloped, the trees that helped sustain these families over the decades still stand on the sides of roads or on the property boundaries in the unused area between pieces of real estate. These are the trees that we have rediscovered. In spite of the fact that they are untended and the fruit goes unharvested, many still produce a decent crop in a good year. Zipping along the roads, on route to one activity or another, we started to notice dozens of these half-feral and neglected apple trees along the sides of the road, and they were full of apples.

Not wanting to turn our noses up at free food, we began picking these apples. They are not the same as the apples you buy in the store. Not perfectly formed or large like those our society has become accustomed to, they can be ugly with black spots. Some might have a resident worm. But, they are delicious and edible. Most of the unsightliness is only skin deep. Peel away the skin, and they

We hit the mother lode of wild apples.

contain beautiful white flesh that rivals anything you could find in our modern food chain. Making no particularly big effort to pick clean each tree or even to get to all we had spied, we harvested near-ly 100 pounds of apples. We were a bit late for some of the trees and figured that we would easily have been able to pick double that amount if we had paid closer attention to the season and the progress of each individual tree.

Apples can have many uses. As well as just eating them, we can applesauce to last over the long year until the next harvest. We have even sliced them and dehydrated them for storage. The wild apples were mostly used to make hard apple cider.

Apples may not fit into the picture for all people as a foraged food, but our definition allows us to take advantage of this amazing food source. For those new to foraging, apples may be a good place to start. Easily recognizable, they can be gathered in large quanti-ties in a relatively short amount of time. We felt a great sense of

Apple Cider Made Easy

A great deal of information is available to those interested in home-brewing, although much centers around manipulating the natural fermentation process. For our purposes, we like to be as minimalist as possible, allowing nature to do most of the work. Our process is a bit unconventional, but works for us and keeps us in cider.

1. Begin by washing the surface dirt and grime from the apples and slicing them into quarters.
2. Feed the quarters into a juicer. We were fortunate enough to find a used juicer for $35 from a local seller on Craigslist.
3. Strain the juice through cheesecloth into a fermenting bucket.
4. Add sugar to raise the potential alcohol content to somewhere in the 7 to 12 percent range, depending on personal preference.
5. Add brewer's yeast. We have used a variety of yeasts in our cider, including ale yeast, which is usually used to make a lower alcohol content beer. Often, our cider is closer to an apple wine, with alcohol content usually between 7 and 14 percent ABV (ciders are typically between 4 and 8 percent ABV).
6. Close it up, using an airlock, and wait for the primary fermentation to stop.

At this point, one has a choice:

7. Transfer the cider into another vessel to clear. This is not necessary unless a cider that is a beautiful, clear golden color is desired. If not, feel free to skip this step.
8. Bottle it, being careful not to get any of the sediment into the bottles. Don't forget to prime the bottle with a bit of sugar to give it a bit of fizz.

The final and most difficult step:

9. Let the cider sit in the bottles for six months or so. ☞

I am not sure that we have ever made it six months. The cider can be consumed a few weeks after the bottling process, but is supposed to mellow to a better flavor over time.

accomplishment when we first started accepting the fruits nature freely offered from the many neglected and abandoned trees.

Our experience of finding wild apples was not our only happy accident. For many years, we wanted to add hazelnut (*Corylus americana*) bushes to our homestead. The goal was to have as many nutritionally and calorie-dense perennial foods as possible, and after researching nut options, hazelnut (a native to our area) seemed the best choice.

We planted several hazelnut bushes on our property at not an inconsiderable cost with regard to the amount of time, effort and actual money spent. When we first started looking for hazelnut bushes, very few local nurseries even had them listed in their catalog, and the ones that did charged a lot for them. Unfortunately, not only did we lose as many of the bushes as we managed to grow, but they have not grown very quickly or ever produced.

Like many homes in New England, ours has an oil burning furnace. Given the lack of a basement, a garage or sufficient room inside the house, the tank for our oil is outside of the house. For years, we carefully mowed around and under the tank to keep down the bramble and such that seem to want to grow there so that our oil delivery person had easier access.

When we started transitioning from oil to wood and stopped getting oil deliveries, keeping the area around the oil tank clear became less of a priority, and at some point, we noticed a woody shrub of some sort was growing out from under the tank. As the shrub grew bigger, we tried numerous times to identify it. At one point, we were certain that it was an elm, which, thanks to Dutch Elm disease, has been all but wiped out in this area. We decided that if it was an elm tree, we needed to be sure to preserve it, and so, while we were not entirely sure of its identity, we left the tree alone for a season.

The next stab at finding out its name resulted in labeling it a birch tree. We were certain that it was a yellow birch, based on the bark and leaves, but it would have to grow a bit bigger before we could accurately determine what it was, and so we left it for another season.

We decided to wait until one of our friends or mentors who were more experienced with plant identification visited our house. Before that could happen, however, we figured it out on our own. We noticed a pod-like flower growing under the leaves, and had an Aha! moment, when we compared the pod on our unknown bush with one of the pods on the bushes we had been trying hard to grow. It was a hazelnut, and of all of the hazelnuts growing in our yard, this was growing the best — the one we had invested nothing more than a passing interest in for several years. It was a very exciting discovery for us.

We mentioned the bush to our neighbor, a long-time area resident who had eked out an existence with his father on a small island off the coast when he was young. He finds us quite quirky and fun to watch, because much of what we are trying to accomplish on our quarter acre reminds him of how he and his father lived on their island. As he chuckled, he mentioned that thirty years ago the whole area, before all of the development, had been covered in blueberries and hazelnuts.

This got the wheels turning, and we started thinking that perhaps this was not some cosmic gag, that maybe other bushes had survived (or regenerated) the suburban sprawl. We began to look more closely at the underbrush in the wild spaces between our yards. In a single five-minute stroll down our road, we found nearly a dozen more hazelnut bushes of various sizes that all had pods. There are probably many more that are not big enough to produce yet.

Unfortunately, the hazelnuts are not quite as prolific as we would like to them to be. That or the competition is just incredibly fierce for this delicacy, because since we successfully and accurately identified our bush and found its brothers along the road, we have only managed to harvest about a dozen nuts.

In years past, our meager harvest was due to our ignorance and failure to pay attention, and, perhaps even more so, to the competition between us and the squirrels, chipmunks and mice, but this year, we thought we had a handle on things. We paid particular attention to the nut development, and even opened up a pod or two before they were ripe to check on the progress. Our youngest daughter counted all of the nuts she could find — about twenty-two on one bush we were really watching — and we estimated when they might be ready for harvest. As the date of harvest neared, we were out of town. On our return, we rushed out to the bush to gather the ripe nuts, excited to, at last, have some roasted hazelnuts, but much to our chagrin, we found that most of the nuts had already been plundered. The rodents won again. We were still able to harvest a few, however, and easily tripled our previous years' record hauls by collecting eight to ten small nuts. These were dried to be ground for adding flavor and texture to a future meal.

We have had much better luck with the other nut tree that lives wild in our area, specifically, the oaks. While they do not give syrup, they do provide acorns — in usually large quantities — and for years, we have talked about processing acorns into flour. After attending classes that gave us an overview of each required step, we had made a very small amount of flour but had not taken the big leap into really processing acorns in quantity.

Some years, there were so few acorns that we simply did not bother, or the trees were generous enough, but we did not have time to gather them, or we gathered them but did not process them before the weevils got them. The latter is most often the case. Interestingly, we have discovered that if one leaves the acorns on the ground, scattered as they fell from the trees, the weevils do not seem to infest them as badly as they do if the acorns are gathered and stored in a bucket, which will usually result in the entire harvest being unfit for us, but a lovely treat for the weevils.

Some literature on acorn collecting will state that certain acorns are better than others — bigger or sweeter or whatever constitutes *better*. As with the maples, we do not have the luxury of being choosy and accepted the oak tree's gift, even if our harvest is not the sweetest or the best possible choice. All oaks provide acorns — all of which can be eaten, but some require a bit more work to process than others.

We have made and used small amounts of acorn flour, but as the nationally recognized Day of Thanks dawned, we woke with a taste of something different.

That morning, I awoke dreaming of making acorn pie. I have a sweet tooth and am fond of pecan pie, but for our harvest meal, we have, for many years, resolved to make it local, and unfortunately pecans are not grown in Maine. When I woke thinking of acorn pie, the first step was to find some sort of recipe, but, oddly enough, acorn pie is not something that very many people crave, and so my search was unrewarded. I switched tactics and decided to look for what I wanted, which was a pecan pie recipe to modify with ingredients that I could locally source. I found a very simple recipe online and began the process of making my substitutions. Instead of pecans, it would be acorns. Instead of corn syrup, it would be honey from our beehive.

I threw on a coat, grabbed a plastic grocery bag and strolled out the door and down the road. I gathered the few acorns that were lying out in the open fairly quickly, inspecting each for freshness and bug holes. With not nearly enough acorns for a pie, I stopped and thought about seeing the clawed-up ground where wild turkeys had searched for food. It reminded me of the way the chickens did the same. I began kicking up the piles of wet, dead leaves on the ground and discovered what the birds already knew, that the tasty morsels I sought were hiding under the leaf litter. In less than a half hour, I gathered three pounds of raw acorns still in their shells.

Returning to the house, I gathered the equipment needed to shell the acorns. I decided that it would be easier to separate the flesh from the shell if I simply quartered the nuts with a knife and peeled the shell off of the remaining meat. We had tried a few other methods, such as smashing them open between two pieces of wood. That worked well, but it was difficult to collect all of the meat from the small pieces of shell. When we tried a nutcracker, we found that the nut had to be lined up exactly or it did not break cleanly. This new quartering method worked well and was quick, or so I thought. After two hours of shelling, I had a bowl full of meat, a bowl full of shells and a dozen or so weevil-infested acorns that were tossed back outside.

The bitterness of acorns makes them unpalatable to humans, which is probably why the squirrels and chipmunks want the hazelnuts as badly as we do. The taste is a result of tannins, which can be leached out of the acorns in several ways. One method (which we have done) involves immersing the shelled acorns in cold running

Processing acorns can take a long time, but the result is worth the effort.

water, like a stream, or letting them soak in cold water for several days with multiple water changes every day.

Because our plan was to use the nuts that day, the best choice for us was the hot-water leaching method, which entails boiling the nut meats in water until the water takes on a brownish red tinge. The brown water and any loose skins floating in the water are poured off, and the nuts are then covered with fresh cold water and boiled again. It took twelve changes of water and five and a half hours to remove most of the tannic acid to a point where the meats were only faintly bitter.

We made a crust using lard rendered from fat we were given with our most recent pig share, and the pie filling was poured into the crust. When the pie came out of the oven, it looked exactly like pecan pie.

Twelve hours after waking up and deciding on acorn pie for our harvest dessert, we were cutting into the slices. The most important thing we always emphasize about foraged foods is that, while some

Who knew acorns could be made into a pie?

foraged foods are *like* a cultivated counterpart, the taste is never exactly the same. Acorn pie is not pecan pie. Acorns are not as sweet or tender as pecans, and honey is not as gooey as corn syrup, but the pie was definitely edible, and it was even good. For our next acorn pie, we will do things a little differently. In particular, we will roast the acorns for a more nutty texture rather than the chewy texture of the ones in our pie.

We used only about half of the processed acorns in the pie. The rest were roasted in the oven while the pie cooked and later ground into flour using a mortar and pestle to break the larger pieces into more manageable chunks and then fed into the hand-crank food mill.

We have several uses for the many different flours we make from roots and nuts that we grow (sunchokes) and forage (acorns), including adding them as thickeners and flavorings to soups, making dumplings, noodles, pancakes or fried flat breads. In our class, where we first learned to process acorns into flour, we made acorn cookies, which were baked on sticks held over an open fire or fried in a pan like hoe-cakes. Unlike wheat flour, acorn flour does not contain gluten, and so it will not rise into a fluffy yeast bread. There are still plenty of tasty ways to use it in our kitchens, and the fact that it is gluten free ... and free ... becomes incredibly appealing as more people find themselves unable to tolerate gluten products.

Sap, fruit and nuts are amazing gifts from the trees, but their generosity does not stop there. Here in the Pine Tree State, there is one more gift from the trees that we have learned to use.

We are primarily tea drinkers. There was a time when coffee was our beverage of choice, and between us, we could consume a couple of pots per day. One of the first small appliances we purchased was an automatic-drip coffee maker. While our everyday tea of choice differs with one of us reaching for the green tea and the other enjoying an herbal brew, there is one tea that both of us will drink. When we have colds or feel them coming on, it is not uncommon for us to have a pot of evergreen tea brewing on the top of the wood stove.

· The needles of evergreens contain high quantities of vitamin C, some sources estimating the contents to be five to ten times higher than that of citrus fruit. Anecdotes from European sailors tell of a miracle drink given to them by the North American natives as a cure for scurvy. Historians believe this drink to have been an evergreen tea.

Evergreen needles also contain high quantities of other vitamins and minerals. For instance, white pine needles are high in vitamin A. White pine tea is renowned as a healing tea, a fact that has even been noted by modern pharmacology. The needles contain the same chemicals that are used as the base for Tamiflu, a drug used to treat and prevent the flu.

White pine is an excellent source of vitamin C.

When we hear grumblings from friends and co-workers about upper respiratory complaints, our first reaction is to recommend white pine tea, which has resulted in the acquisition of a reputation at work of being a crunchy nature freak. Reactions vary, of course, from admissions that the person does not know what white pine is or where to get it, to questions about how to make the tea or how it tastes.

One co-worker mentioned the tea to his wife, who in the past had been on prescription asthma medication. She tried the tea and decided that she liked the taste. She claims using white pine helped her get off her medication, and whether or not it was the tea, she has continued to enjoy it, because she liked the flavor.

While we use it primarily as a preventive or curative, it is a delicious tea that fills the house with the wonderful smell of the pine forest. This pleasantly sweet tea is good either by itself or with a bit of added sugar or honey.

When we feel the need of a little immunity boost during the winter, we will fill a large pot with leaves, cover it with water and simmer it on the back of the wood stove. We use not only white pine, but also eastern hemlock (*Tsuga canadensis*) (a tree that should not be confused with the water hemlock plant (*Cicuta*), which is not edible) and spruce boughs, and as we remove cups of tea or as the water evaporates, we add more. When the tea starts getting too weak, we put the soggy branches in the compost, and depending on whether we still feel the need for the healing tonic, we will forage more leaves and make a new batch.

There are very few plants that we know to gather during the winter. Of them, evergreen tea is one, and since the leaves are ever present, there is no need to gather large quantities and store it. Nature will take care of that for you.

We might have stopped at evergreen tea had we not discovered Stephen Buhner's book *Sacred and Herbal Healing Beers*.[4] As luck would have it, our neighbors were thinning out some trees on their property and decided that the stand of spruce trees needed to go. In exchange for cutting down the tree, they told us we could keep it to use as a Christmas tree. It was a bit tall for our living room, so we had to cut off a considerable portion. Not wanting to waste the branches, we decided to try the recipe in Mr. Buhner's book for spruce beer.

Making spirits is fairly simple. The basic recipe is to make a tea, add sugar, add yeast (or allow wild yeast to settle), put the mixture into an airlock and wait. This spruce beer recipe called for molasses as the sugar, and so the beer was very dark and rich with a strong licorice flavor (from the molasses). The fifty bottles was a bit much, and our lesson in making that brew was that smaller batches, and perhaps a different sugar, would be better.

After the ease of making spruce beer, we decided to try making beer from eastern hemlock. We made a very strong tea and added sugar to achieve about 7 percent ABV and cider yeast. The resulting beer was much lighter than its spruce counterpart.

We are continually learning from the trees, and we know there is more to explore about other trees. Up the road, about a mile from our house, is a stand of basswood (also known as linden or *Tilia americana*) trees that offers a whole slew of gifts, including the inner bark, which can be used as cordage, the flowers which can be made into a fragrant tea, and the leaves, which we are told can be consumed as a salad. In fact, our teachers once dubbed the basswood their "lettuce tree," because they routinely pick the early leaves for a salad.

Young beech leaves and maple leaves are also, reportedly, edible. Birch trees (of which there are very few in our immediate area) can be tapped for syrup that has a distinctly wintergreen flavor. We are hoping to find an autumn olive, which is an invasive, and our favorite thing to do with invasive plants is to eat them.

With much still to learn from the trees, we are certain that our lessons will never be complete in our lifetimes. While we are still learning, however, we will remain incredibly thankful for the gifts we receive from the trees.

Acorn Pie**

1 9-inch pie crust
2½ cups leached acorns, chopped (and roasted)
½ cup butter
½ cup honey
½ cup raw cane sugar
¼ cup heavy cream
¼ tsp salt

1. Preheat oven to 350°F.
2. Roll out crust and put into pie pan.

*The recipe recommends baking the crust before adding the filling; we opted not to follow this step.

3. Melt butter in a medium sauce pan. Add honey, sugar, cream and salt and stir until sugar completely dissolves.
4. Allow mixture to cool to room temperature.
5. Add acorns to butter mixture.
6. Pour acorn mixture into pie crust.
7. Place filled pie pan on a cookie sheet in the middle of oven and bake until the filling is bubbling vigorously, including the middle, about 40 minutes.
8. Allow pie to cool and set before serving.

**adapted from Classic Pecan Pie recipe: http://localfoods.about.com/od/piestarts/r/Pecan-Pie.htm

CHAPTER 6

Fauna

I N OUR READING AND RESEARCH, we have found that foraging books
generally do not touch on animal sources of food. In fact, most
people would not consider meat a foraged food. We have tried dozens of dietary transitions in our lifetimes, including vegetarianism,
but the one that finally makes the most sense to us is eating locally.
At first, that meant what we could buy or raise locally, but at some
point, we realized that, the most responsible, most sustainable diet
for us had to be food that naturally occurred in our local area. It was
simple reasoning. First, if imported food were to be less available
or become too expensive, we would need to eat what we could find
locally anyway. Second, it made sense to us that the food that was
available at any given time of year would provide the exact nutrients
we needed for that time of year in our climate.

The first step toward having a truly local diet was to figure out
what the people who lived here before Europeans arrived ate. Kerry
Hardy's book, *Notes on a Lost Flute: A Field Guide to the Wabanaki,*[1]
has a section on the native diet. What it shows is that the natives
who lived in what is now Maine, for thousands of years before the
Europeans landed Down East, were omnivores. In modern Maine

and climates like ours, there are growing concerns about vitamin D deficiency, which nearly everyone in my climate has, we are discovering. The best way to get this essential vitamin is by sun exposure, but in Maine, during the winter, the sun is too low on the horizon to be an effective source. In addition, when it is cold out, people tend to not be out as much, and when they are, too much of their skin is covered to allow the kind of exposure that would be necessary to get an adequate supply of vitamin D.

Whether or not they were aware of vitamin deficiencies, a quick look at the natives' diet shows that their seasonal/local diet gave them the best sources of the vitamins necessary for good health. If vitamin D cannot be acquired through exposure to the sun, the next best source is fish. During the winter, freshwater eels were a big part of the native diet.

When first transitioning our diet to what we could find locally, we did so with the goal of ensuring that we would have the best, most well-rounded, healthiest diet possible — without the need for taking manufactured supplements. Part of a well-rounded diet, for us, includes meat, and fortunately, because we live in Maine, we have many wild options available. Although we raise rabbits and chickens for meat, neither of us has a lot of experience in hunting or fishing. We did not have a lot of experience with wild foraging plants either, and so this was not much of a deterrent.

Neither of us grew up hunting or fishing, although we both have family members who hunted. Grandfathers and uncles were hunters, and an annual Thanksgiving Day hunt was normal as an after-dinner excursion at Grammy's house. Fishing was a favored activity of some of our southern relatives, but was a mind-numbingly boring activity that was never fully appreciated by the impatient youths we were. While relatives did hunt and fish regularly, killing animals was just not a part of our youth experiences.

For whatever reason, I took up hunting with a bow about four years ago. I am not sure why, but it felt right. I bought an old used compound bow from e-Bay and practiced shooting it in the back yard. I practiced with co-workers who had shot bows throughout their lives. I learned to tune it properly and changed the sights and rests to suit my style. I attended the local bow hunter safety course and got my first hunting license.

Learning to use the weapon was given priority, especially early in my hunting experience, and I assumed, perhaps like many novices, that knowing how to use my tool was all that was necessary to prepare myself for a successful hunt. Over the years, I learned that an equally important part of the hunting experience is developing skills in scouting and tracking. I have learned that knowing the area, being able to tell if the target animal has been in the area — recently — and being patient and quiet while in the woods are just as (maybe more) important than being an expert shot. After three years of being a licensed bow hunter, all of the skills, finally, came together to produce results.

We do raise some of our own meat on our tiny quarter acre homestead, but because of our limited space, we cannot raise large animals such as cows and pigs. While most of our protein comes from the chickens and rabbits we raise (and even in our small space, we have raised all of the roasting chickens and rabbit that we have eaten for the past several years), I have tended to focus on deer hunting, although my original intent was to hunt turkey.

My regular job tends to get in the way of making real strides in hunting, particularly bow hunting. The scouting portion of hunting, that is being out in the woods — just walking around, getting to know the area, and looking for signs of what animals might live there — is an essential part of the hunting experience. Without knowing where the animals are, one cannot hope to make them a meal. This requires a great deal of time in the woods to scout out suitable locations. Unfortunately, juggling a full-time job and working toward a hand-made life makes time a very precious commodity. With hunting season occurring in the fall, the exact same time as winding down the homestead and getting it ready for winter (chopping wood, closing up garden beds, preparing chicken coops and greenhouses for snow, etc.), very little time is left to devote to pre-season scouting. So, when I noticed that a rather healthy-looking and populous rafter (the official term for a flock of turkeys) had moved into our neighborhood, hanging around the same area at roughly the same time each day, I decided that my focus should be on securing a turkey.

I watched them. In the morning, they waddled out of the woods and paraded up our dirt lane toward the main road that borders our property. They would forage in the tall grass next to the lane, as they made their way into our neighbor's yard. After a few minutes pecking around in the field across from us, they would file into our yard to see what they could find for breakfast among the spent gardens and flowers gone to seed.

After a week or two, I noticed that they seemed to have a routine of coming up the road in the morning, visiting the neighbor to the west, traveling through our yard and jumping the fence into our eastern neighbor's yard. Then they headed into the brook, back through the small patch of woods and into the large development down the road, where they would spend the day foraging and soaking up the sunshine. In the evening, they reversed their routine. One night, after their daily migration through our yard, I followed them down the lane to discover that they were roosting in the pines behind our neighbor's house. I decided that I would hunt them the next morning.

I woke later than I wanted and looked out quickly only to see the rafter walking straight toward me. I hurried to find my tools, and carefully selected the arrow, winding the broadhead tip onto the shaft. As I eased into position, I scouted the flock, identifying a young tom that would be the best candidate for our table, and then waited calmly for the bird to come into range. It waddled off in the other direction, but a juvenile hen passed right into the perfect position. I exhaled and loosed.

The arrow passed right through the base of her neck across the top of her heart, severing all of the arteries, and exited through her chest. She died where she had last stood without running or flying away. I was thankful that the kill was clean and mercifully quick. I walked to where she lay exhaling her last breath to express my thanks to her for the incredible gift she was giving.

The turkey hen looked good sized, but weighed just over six pounds. Small though she was (some of the roosters we raise over the summer are larger), she was the culmination of years of effort. My first year of hunting, I got within range of several deer, but had not taken a shot, in an effort to ensure that I was able to get the perfect shot. I did not relax my personal ethical standards to make this shot, rather I have simply become confident in my ability to take the shot and know that the animal would not suffer unnecessarily.

The turkey hen helped complete my education as a hunter. I had to follow through with all of the required steps, legally and ethically: taking the shot, watching her die, bringing her to the tagging station, plucking her, gutting her, putting her in the freezer and finally making an offering of thanks to the rest of the flock.

She also reinforced a very important lesson for successful hunting — scouting. I had always thought that scouting meant spending time in the woods before the season opened to look for signs that the animals were in the area. Actually, it means knowing where the animals will be and when. This flock had been hanging around my neighborhood for the better part of a month. I watched them make their early morning circuit each day scratching around for food, and I also discovered where they spent their nights.

Finally, she reminded me of some basic hunting practices. Specifically, I was reminded to move slowly and remain calm. Whether they are responding to our emotions, some unconscious body language or something else entirely, animals seem to be able to sense extremes of emotion, and they will react. Being very conscious of my movements, my breathing and my emotions helped to keep my calm, to keep the adrenaline rush in check. Without that rush, there was no sense of urgency that causes mistakes — just calm, quiet stillness.

She helped dispel a few myths for me, too. As with many other aspects of my life, I tend to keep things simple. I do not get bogged down with the idea that I need the newest equipment or the latest technologies, like scent-lock clothing and a 320 fps bow with a slick release. Normally when hunting, I wear an old pair of BDUs (Battle Dress Uniform, the camouflage uniform worn by soldiers) from my time in the Army. I "fingers" shoot an old 90s vintage Hoyt compound bow. On the morning I stalked the turkey hen, I had thrown on a pair of jeans, a t-shirt and a fleece and pulled on a pair of worn hiking boots. I did not try to hide from the flock by masking my scent or camouflaging myself.

The six-pound turkey hen was the centerpiece of our Thanksgiving meal. Of the many ways we could have prepared her, we decided to season the meat with a blend of salt and herbs and roast her on our grill over a bed of smoke chips. The smoked turkey was incredibly tender and delicious, and tasted absolutely nothing like store-bought,

We were surprised that the turkeys visited our yard this year.

factory-farmed turkey. We had enough meat for our family of five and canned an additional two quarts of meat and bone broth.

The suburbs where we live in southern Maine are rich with wild-life. The woods are teeming with all sorts of animals that we could have eaten, including raccoon (which sometimes try to compete with us for our backyard chickens), opossum, birds of all kinds, squirrel, porcupine, whistle pig (also known as groundhog, which sometimes tries to compete with us for our garden fare), skunk, deer, fox, coyote and fishers, to name a few that we have actually seen. Many others are indigenous to our area, which we have not seen, but are very likely out there. In addition, we are surrounded by small streams and ponds, and there are a couple of rivers within a reasonable distance where we could find all sorts of fish and other aquatic life forms.

Hunting and fishing are both regulated by the State, however, and since we did not have fishing equipment, we opted not to apply for a fishing license. We had hoped to learn something about lobstering and even talked about getting a couple of traps, but the rules state that lobster traps must be set from a boat, which we do not have.

If the turkey had been the only meat we had been gifted for the year, we would have considered the hunting part of our beginner hunter/gather lifestyle a success. Luckily for us, we did not have to settle for just the turkey. Living on the coast, we could have fished without a license from the beach (depending on the beach and the time of year, as some local ordinances prohibit fishing from the beach during the tourist-heavy months). Again, being limited by the lack of equipment, we did no saltwater fishing either.

What did happen was a completely new and completely outra-geous and completely amazing experience with learning to dig for clams on the tidal flats. We have some friends who actually go clam-ming. It is quite a well-respected pastime among the many outdoorsy natives who make up our circle of friends and acquaintances. When we talked with one particular friend, about our project, he offered to take us clamming. Unfortunately, our schedules never seemed to sync, and so he was unable to give us a tutorial on how to best go about the process. Which did not stop us from attempting to clam on our own.

We briefly discussed what equipment was needed and decided that we did not want to spend the $75 or more on a clamming fork. We figured the local indigenous people, who surely enjoyed the occasional clam feast, did not have expensive clamming forks. From what we could find, a native digging tool was a stick, and so we figured if it was good enough for them, it was good enough for us. We should be okay with minimal to no fancy tools.

One bright, sunny Sunday afternoon, armed only with a couple of buckets for the massive haul of clams we expected to bring home, we checked the tide charts to find out when it would be low tide, made sure that we were not experiencing a red tide (which is an overgrowth of bacteria that makes the clams toxic) and headed out to find the evening's dinner.

Tidal flats are pretty interesting places. Half a day, the mud is buried under the water. The other half, it bakes in the sun, and so when it is exposed, the ground looks firm and treadable to the untrained eye. The solid-looking mud is littered with stuff the tide leaves behind, driftwood, seaweed and what looks like seashells. Upon closer inspection, we realized that those seashells were actually snails and tried to avoid walking on them. Rocks exposed as the waters retreated are covered with tiny periwinkles, and we avoided stepping on those, also.

The ground looks solid enough, but after three or four steps, the sponge-like mud sucks around one's foot and calf like quicksand. The first time (not the day we went clamming, thankfully) we walked onto the salt flats, I nearly lost a shoe, and my daughters, who were very young then, were terrified of sinking knee deep in the muck.

The day of our clamming adventure, we already knew about the sucking mud flats and did not wear our shoes as we waded out to find our treasures. We knew nothing, however, about finding clams.

Some anecdotal tales reported that the air holes the clams suppos-edly left on the surface would indicate where they were hiding just beneath the mud.

Noting that the sand was making a popping noise like breakfast cereal, we stopped and decided to dig. After a couple of tries with the stick, it broke in two places. Well, sticks are out. We dug into the sand with our bare hands. Digging barehanded, however, proved much more difficult than our mud-encased feet would suggest. The mud is not soft. Trying to dig the layers of deposited silt is like trying to pull up a fist full of wet concrete. There's a reason that a clam fork was invented.

We had been instructed by our friend to dig a trench about one foot square. He told us that the clams would be between two and six inches below the surface. We noticed that our hole was much deeper than this, but we saw no clams. We stopped and looked around and discovered that we were standing on the top of a high spot in the middle of the clam flats. Clever us, we moved to another "crackling sand" area nearer the level of the low tide waters and resumed the dig.

At first, we did not find any clams, but we did find these alien-looking, centipede-like, wormy creatures that tweaked every single gross-out button in our bodies. We later learned these are called bris-tle worms, and they are truly creepy … and they bite. They also eat clams — another fact we learned only after discovering them.

After about an hour (or two) of digging, we had two one-foot by three-feet trenches and what seemed to us a pretty respectable clam harvest. Certainly not what a professional (or an amateur with better equipment) would have found in that same time period, but as nov-ice clammers, we had not done too badly. We decided to call it a day.

Our hands were raw, our legs were sore, and our backs were aching, both from bending over to dig and from the inadvertently exposed skin that ended up sunburned. We slogged through the muck to rinse our clams in the tidal river. After swishing water around in the bucket and pouring out the sandy residue a few times, we noticed that there were a bunch of half shells in the bucket.

How did those get in there?

We took the half shells out of the bucket and continued cleaning the clams in the river water. A few minutes later, we looked into the bucket and saw a couple more half shells.

What the ...?

From more than a dozen clams, we were down to a seven or eight left in the bucket. We reached in and inspected all of the remaining clams and were introduced to "mud clams." A mud clam is a dead clam shell that is filled with mud. After inspecting all of the clams and discarding all of the remaining mud clams, we were left with four clams, which weighed in at a whopping half of a pound.

We made a couple of decisions at that moment when we realized that two hours' work had yielded such a small return. First, four

Initially our clam harvest looked a lot more impressive than it actually was.

clams was good enough for the day. A little protein is better than none, but like the Gambler, we needed to know when to walk away. And second, and probably more importantly, we vowed that when we went back out in search of clams, it would only be if we could be accompanied by someone with both experience and equipment.

We gathered up our daughters and our clams, discovered that the frog pond, where we had hoped to gather some cattails (*Typha*), was home to leeches, and checked on the milkweed and blackberries as we made our way back to our car.

At home, we cleaned and boiled the clams, cut them up and added them to a chowder. The four clams gave us about a pint of soup, and while the exercise may not have provided more than an appetizer for our family, it certainly provided an introductory education to clamming. Next time, we knew a lot more, and sometimes the lesson is more important than the outcome.

What we lack in education and experience, we more than make up for in gumption, and a willingness to put ourselves out there. We know a lot more today than we did a year ago, and each new lesson has empowered us with a deeper understanding of how capable we are, if we allow ourselves to simply learn, without fear.

Wild turkey, from now on, will be part of our harvest meal, and if we can serve a clam chowder as an appetizer, all the better.

CHAPTER 7

Fungi

LATER IN THE SEASON, as autumn sets in, one can easily observe mushrooms throughout the landscape. They grow on trees, in fields and in the seemingly barren clutter under the trees. When walking through the woods, we always noticed the rainbow of colorful mushrooms dotting the forest floor, from the LBM (little brown mushrooms) to psychedelically colored purple, orange and red varieties.

Our children learned to respect mushrooms as part of the Faery world (a ring of mushrooms marked a Faery ring and was special and best left undisturbed). We enjoyed finding them and carefully studying the many little capped fungi littering the forest floor, but we knew we did not have enough information to pick any of them.

As much as we have learned about other plants to forage, we are complete neophytes when it comes to the mushroom world. There are hundreds of thousands, perhaps millions, of species of mushrooms in the world. We have read that nearly two-thirds are inedible, dozens of which can be fatally toxic. While Maine probably has only a few hundred varieties of mushrooms, maybe a few dozen that are suitable for a meal, the learning curve seemed unbelievably, and unattainably, steep. There is just so much to learn before one can even feel mildly comfortable attempting to forage what is probably the most complicated of wild foods.

In general, society has a significant phobia when it comes to mushrooms. Nearly every person we have spoken with about foraging mushrooms, and nearly every book we have read, has warned us that we need to be very careful, because mushrooms are deadly. There are mushrooms, and there are toad stools. The fungi can have caps, or not, and gills, or not. Sometimes there is a bulb at the base of the mushroom, and sometimes just a smooth stem. And all of these little nuances can give us some indication as to the edibility of the mushroom we have discovered.

We knew we needed mushrooms to be a part of our diet, whether foraged or not. Many species of mushrooms are coveted for their incredible healing properties. In addition, they are nutritionally and calorie dense, and if our diet was going to be local, seasonal and foraged, we needed to get the biggest bang for our buck. Our diet had to include mushrooms.

At first, we tried to grow our own. We started with a box of portabella mushroom spore and harvested several very large mushrooms and a few very small ones, which were incredibly delicious as only fresh homegrown food can be. Once all the spore in the box had matured into a mushroom, which we picked and ate, the box stopped producing mushrooms and became just a box of dirt in the corner. In order to keep growing this particular crop, we learned that we would have to buy a new box.

Instead, we seeded oak logs with inoculated plugs of shiitake. It took nearly eighteen months before we were able to harvest our first three pounds of mushrooms from our logs. The next year, following a dry, cold winter and a fairly hot, dry summer, we did not harvest any at all. Then, in the spring, we were ready to chop the logs up for firewood, but instead threw them into the tiny brook that runs behind our house. Apparently, what they needed was the good soaking, and during the summer, we were able to gather around two pounds of shiitake mushrooms.

Inspired by our varied successes at mushroom growing, we signed up for a workshop that included a hands-on exercise to seed a bag with blue oyster mushrooms. Per instructions, we placed the bag in a sunny, south-facing window in our home, and waited. Two crops of mushrooms were harvested before the mycelium mildewed, molded and turned green. At the workshop, we were told that we might enjoy a couple of crops, but each would get smaller.

The frustration for us with each of these different mushroom growing set-ups was that spore would need to be purchased to start each new batch. Even the shiitake logs would, eventually, go sterile. While none of our mushroom growing experiences required a great deal of space or time, our ultimate goal is to be as self-sufficient as possible and needing to purchase mushroom spore seemed to be counter to this. If mushrooms were to be part of our diet, we needed to learn to identify and harvest them in the wild.

While studying different mushrooms, we found a lot of research regarding the health benefits of eating mushrooms. In addition to being packed with vitamins, proteins and antioxidants, each mushroom we read about has anti-tumor, anti-cancer, immune-boosting, anti-viral, cholesterol-lowering or some other amazing super-food properties. As such, more and more it seemed that the benefits of foraging mushrooms easily outweighed any real risk involved with harvesting and eating them, and learning to find these elusive gourmet delights rocketed up to the top of our to-do list.

The first step in learning as much as we could about foraging mushrooms was to attend some workshops. One of the first we attended focused on medicinal mushrooms, particularly with regard to tree mushrooms or polypore. We were told that all polypore mushrooms that grow in Maine are medicinal ... and more importantly, not poisonous. In addition, since a polypore is usually very tree specific, identifying them is a bit easier if one also knows how to identify native (or local) trees.

Our first real attempt at finding polypore on our own was our search for chaga, which inadvertently resulted in our discovery of wintergreen. We chose chaga because it was very distinctive. First, it usually only grows on live birch trees. It is not believed to be parasitic, although it looks like a huge burned (or wounded) spot on the tree. The black exterior of the chaga contrasts sharply with the white bark of the birch tree, which should make it easy to spot, especially in the fall and winter when there are no leaves on the trees.

Harvesting chaga from the host tree requires some muscle and/ or a good knife. There does not appear to be any harm to either the chaga or the tree following a harvest. In fact, the chaga seems to continue to grow after it has been harvested.

To use chaga, it needs to be dried, but once dry, like most polypores, it becomes rock-hard and difficult to break. Aficionados recommend breaking larger pieces into smaller chunks, which accelerates the drying process and makes using it later a bit easier.

We have used the dried mushroom to make a wonderful tea that is the color of coffee but has a very mild, almost sweet, flavor. With a tiny bit of sugar and a splash of milk or cream, it tastes a bit like warm vanilla milk. During the winter, our most likely time to drink chaga tea, we will put a piece of dried chaga in a pan with water and leave it on the back of the wood stove, allowing it to just steep. Each time we take a cup of tea, we add a bit of water. When the tea starts to lighten in color, we replace the chaga in the pan.

We have also used chaga with other herb combinations for different flavors, as desired. One of our favorite experiments involved combining it with lavender to make a tea, and then, when it had cooled, adding sugar and a SCOBY (symbiotic colony of bacteria and yeast, also called a "Mother") to make kombucha, a fermented tea drink. The resulting effervescent soft drink tasted a bit like peach soda.

Polypores are highly valued for their medicinal qualities. Birch polypore (*Piptoporus betulinus*) reportedly has anti-microbial properties. It was even found on the famous Otzi, the Ice Man, who is thought to have used it to treat intestinal parasites. We have not used birch polypore medicinally for ourselves, but when it looked like our dog might have ingested something that made him want to do what we refer to as the butt drag dance across the carpeting, we started giving him a bit of birch polypore in his food. After a month or so, he stopped his funny little dance, and while we cannot verify if he had parasites or if the polypore was beneficial to him at all, something changed for the better. He is certainly not as uncomfortable as he seemed.

We also learned that aside from being a great super-food, polypores can be used to hold a coal. Some of the literature suggested that natives in our area would put a coal into the polypore, thereby allowing them to transport a piece of their fire, which would save time trying to produce a coal through friction at their next campsite. We inadvertently experimented with this property of chaga when a piece was left on the top of our hot wood stove and started smoldering in the middle of the night. We smelled the smoke before any damage was done, and indeed, the piece of polypore on the wood stove was too small to cause a fire, but it did smolder, emitting a not entirely pleasant odor, and we could have carried it outside and, with a good tinder bundle, started a campfire.

Polypores have many wonderful healthful and useful benefits, but while they are, reportedly, not poisonous, they are not very desired as food. While the teas are wonderful, the woody texture of polypores makes them not very useful as a food, which means that, if polypores were the only mushrooms we could identify, it would not give us much in the way of providing the calories we need.

As such, we knew we needed to learn a bit more about the mushrooms that thrived under the trees. For us, the first step in most of our learning processes seems to be buying a new book. As the philosopher Erasmus is attributed as saying, *When I get money, I buy books. If any is left over, I buy food and clothing.* In our minds, buying books on how to forage covered us for having a book and having food.

We found a great book on identifying wild mushrooms in New England written by Maine native and long-time mushroom forager David Spahr. His book *Edible and Medicinal Mushrooms of New England and Eastern Canada: A Photographic Guidebook to Finding and Using Key Species*[1] includes dozens of beautiful color pictures and great explanations. However, like trying to use any of the several foraging books we own, we became quickly overwhelmed with the abundance of information.

The next logical step, therefore, was to find a teacher or a mentor. Through our permaculture meet-up group, we signed up for a mushroom walk with an honest-to-goodness mycologist. As it turns out, the mycologist is not only an expert at identifying wild edible mushrooms, but he also forages wild gourmet mushrooms for local restaurants. We attended his walks with the goal of learning one mushroom. Just one, because we knew that trying to absorb everything he said would result in our learning nothing, and ultimately make the walk a waste of our time.

Several mushrooms are easily identifiable. Among these are the "foolproof four," which are considered very easy to identify and have very few poisonous look-alikes. We have eaten none of these four: puffballs (*Calvatia gigantean*), chanterelles (*Cantharellus cibarius*), morels (*Morchella*) and chicken of the woods (*Laetiporus sulphureus*). In our mushroom walk, we learned to identify chanterelles, which are a pretty orange color and smell like apricots, but have not yet found chanterelles on our own in the wild.

Our first successful mushroom foray happened as a bit of a fluke. One afternoon in late September or early October, as I walked along a trail I had followed many times before, I noticed some black funnel-shaped mushrooms. They looked familiar, and I thought they might be black trumpet mushrooms (*Craterellus cornucopioides*), but I needed to consult a few resources. Noting the location, I resolved to return if my hunch proved correct and went back to my computer to verify its identity. Once I confirmed that they were, indeed, black trumpets, I hurried back and picked a small boxful of the delicate morsels.

When I got back home, I carefully washed them and dehydrated them. Because of their very thin, fleshy cap, they dried very quickly, and of course, once dried, they store very well. Throughout the winter, we crumble the dried mushrooms in soup stock, over roasts and into scrambled eggs to add a bit of flavor and nutrients. The nicest part about using the dried mushrooms is that, sometimes, children tend to be very particular about what they claim they will eat, and crumbling dried mushrooms over their food hides what might seem weird or unpalatable. Our children, who have convinced themselves that they do not like mushrooms, have no problems eating the foods with added dried mushrooms.

The fall (or spring, for morels) is the time for mushroom harvesting, although like many things, the window of opportunity for finding the edible morsels is very tiny. Some weeks after finding the black trumpet mushrooms, I happened to be walking through a small stand of trees, when I noticed a huge clump of mushrooms growing at the base of an oak.

While I had no idea what I had discovered, it was pretty exciting to see this huge clump. As with the black trumpets, I thought there might be a chance that what I had found was edible, and I thought it might be hen of the woods, or *maitake* (*Grifola frondosa*). I rushed back to my computer to do a quick search and was pretty confident in my identification. Back at the patch, I harvested a five-and-a-half-pound clump.

Maitake is well-known and coveted in Asia for its health benefits. In Japan, it is widely favored for its medicinal properties and is used to balance body systems. It has been attributed with anti-tumor properties, like the chaga, and several other benefits. In addition, it is one of Japan's major culinary mushrooms, used in a wide variety of dishes, including being a key ingredient in some stews and soups, or baked in foil with butter.

Hen of the woods mushrooms, also known as maitake.

Just to be certain of the identification, I sent a description and photo of my find to a couple of mycologists with whom we had worked, and both confirmed that it was hen of the woods. I was very excited about the find, and through a bit more research have discovered that it is possible to find even larger clumps than mine.

We carefully washed the mushroom before cooking a bit in butter and garlic for a quick snack and to taste it. The rest we cut into chunks and put in the freezer. Through the winter, we put them in soups, like chicken, to give it a hardier stock, sautéed them in butter to add to eggs, or used them in stir-fries.

The five-pound chunk of hen of the woods was nearly 900 calories, not including any oil or butter used in cooking. Between the calorie boost and the nutritional power punch provided by the mushrooms, we are thrilled by the find, and it reinforced our goal of learning more about identifying wild mushrooms. We know that we are still not even advanced enough at mushroom foraging to call ourselves amateurs, but we are confident with the few mushrooms that we do know how to identify.

Out of curiosity, we decided to check out the cost of the mushrooms we had found for free out in the woods. Dried black trumpet mushrooms sell for nearly $100 per pound at our local grocery store. And the *maitake*? A gourmet mushroom site sells hen of the woods for $18 per pound online. We harvested $90 worth of hen of the woods and got a great deal — powerfully nutritious food that cost only the amount of time we were willing to devote to finding it.

We have an extremely limited knowledge of mushrooms, and like every expert (which we are not and do not pretend to be) and every mushroom foraging book (which this is not) cautions, one should never harvest and eat any plant without first being 100 percent sure of what it is. Before we ate any of our foraged mushrooms, we consulted at least three resources.

Finding wild food is incredibly rewarding, and we know that mushrooms will remain a part of our experience as foragers.

Hen of the Woods Soup

3 tbsp butter
4 cloves garlic, crushed
1 lb wild mushrooms, cut into pieces
¼ cup sherry or white cooking wine
2 cups chicken broth
Salt, to taste

1. Melt butter in a heavy pan.
2. Add garlic and mushrooms and cook until mushrooms are tender.
3. Add cooking wine and simmer for five minutes.
4. Add broth and allow to simmer for fifteen minutes so that the flavors blend.
5. Salt to taste.

Fresh or dried greens and herbs can be added to the soup for more flavor.

Part II

Why We Decided to Start Foraging

After we discovered how much rose hips cost in the grocery store, we decided to forage the free ones.

CHAPTER 8

Food Safety and Security

W E SPENT A LOT OF YEARS LOOKING FOR PLANTS to add to our permaculture-inspired garden. The idea behind permaculture is to use perennial edibles for landscaping rather than ornamental plants usually found in urban and suburban landscapes. Ideally, the perennials chosen will be native to the area. The brilliance behind using edible perennials is that they are lower maintenance than annuals (i.e., they do not have to be reseeded every year), and they serve the multiple functions of adding beauty (a key impetus for landscaping at all), providing shade from the sun or shelter from winds, serving as a ground cover to prevent erosion and producing food — for both animals and humans.

Many commonly used edible perennials adorn our parks and public spaces, like apple and cherry trees, whose blossoms are a joy in the spring (although, ironically, the fruit is often viewed as an annoyance in the fall). Dozens of flowers are both beautiful and edible, like *Rosa rugosa* with its edible petals and hips. There are also nut trees and berry bushes, ornamental edible greens (like kale) and dozens of herbs, including fun plants that are also delicious like rosemary (an evergreen in warmer climates) and artichokes (not to be confused with sunchokes, a.k.a Jerusalem artichoke, which are different, but also edible).

Taking advantage of semi-wild foods (i.e., those grown for ornamental purposes and not strictly for food), while a fairly new concept for most of us here in the Western world, is a fairly common practice elsewhere. We heard this story about a Westerner who was visiting in Southeast Asia and remarked about how straight and neat the stands of bamboo were cut. The Westerner marveled at what careful gardeners they must be to keep their landscaping so carefully pruned, to which the local chuckled, stating that it was quite the contrary. Locals knew that young bamboo shoots are both nutritious and delicious, and any growing outside the fence line were public property. It was not the homeowners' efforts to keep the sidewalks clear, but rather passers-by who discovered dinner. In parts of the world, where food scarcity is an issue, foraging is both accepted and expected.

Here in the US, so many people are afraid, because of their lack of knowledge or because they do not want to get into trouble or maybe some combination of both. There is a park near our local library, and a few years ago, their groundskeeper started seeding annual edibles among the mostly inedible ornamentals. Once, when talking with the librarian, we commented on how incredible it was that the groundskeeper was adding these edibles to the landscape design, and how well they seemed to fit in with their neighbors. She stated that it was entirely intentional, and that his hope was that people in need would harvest the plants and take them home for a good meal. Very few of the plants were harvested, because while some people might have recognized the plants, they did not know if it was okay to harvest them.

There are half a dozen apples trees in that same park. Several years ago, we were in the park with some new acquaintances, one a teenaged boy. I pointed out the apples, and he asked, "Can you eat them?" I said, "Yes, of course." All apples are edible, but I cautioned that it was still early, and they might not taste very good. They didn't — taste very good, that is — but the teenager was surprised that these apples were food. Real food. Just growing right there. He then asked, "Can we pick them?" To that I had to admit ignorance, because I did not know what "they" — those faceless authorities to whom we often give so much control — intended to do with the apples. My best guess was nothing, but I still do not know for certain, although I am more likely, these days, to pick the apples with or without permission, as it is a public park. Without any posted commentary to the contrary, I assume that, as part of the taxpaying public, as long as I am respectful and follow the Forager's Rule of Thirds, I can take what I need.

Way back, even before permaculture became the rage, when starting to landscape our quarter acre, we had already decided that everything planted had to be edible and/or medicinal. While some pretty flowers would have been nice, we knew that we could not devote precious space to plants that would only feed our eyes. So, when we started researching what to grow in the garden, one of the plants we sought was Jerusalem artichoke. All we knew, in the beginning, was that it had some amazing nutritional qualities and could be made into flour. What we have since learned was a lot more remarkable. First, we discovered that Jerusalem artichoke, contrary to the name, did not originate in the Middle East. In fact, Jerusalem artichoke, also known as sunchokes, is a native to North America, more specifically, to the northeast. It is also nothing like the familiar globe artichoke (*Cynara cardunculus*), which is a flower (not native to Maine and does not grow well in our short growing season), but rather is an energy-rich, calorie-dense tuber that resembles ginger root. The stalks can grow twenty feet tall, topped by a beautiful, tiny, bright yellow sunflower. It blooms in the fall and adds a brilliance to the changing landscape tapestry.

The Europeans who arrived on the North American shores and first met the natives were introduced to a plethora of amazing plant foods, many of which they took back home. Anyone who has ever planted sunchokes can assume what happened as soon as the roots were dropped into European soil. They grew ... and grew ... and grew ... and grew. Sunchokes grow on a rhizome and are incredibly invasive and prolific. Six tubers can, over the course of one season, become a five-foot by five-foot patch. For whatever reason, sunchokes never gained the kind of popularity that made them into a common food like so many of the other crops introduced to the settlers by the natives and so they remained an obscure (exotic?) vegetable not commonly eaten by most people in America.

Until we started researching our perennial garden options, we did not know anything about sunchokes. Even today, many people we speak with have never heard of them. In spite of how easily they grow and how healthful they have been proven to be, especially for people on glycemic-restricted diets (like those with diabetes), sunchokes are not part of the usual American diet.

What happened in this country, especially since the Industrial Revolution, was that wild foods were deemed of lesser quality, and therefore less desirable, than cultivated foods. The prevailing attitude seemed to become that if one had to forage for food, that meant that one was too poor to purchase food, and in this Land of Opportunity, where everyone could and should be rich, being poor was akin to being worthless and lazy. Only those who were very desperate foraged, and only in times of extreme hardship ... or only for certain foods.

Some wild foods are still favored delicacies. Certain herbs, like wild ginseng (*Panax ginseng*), are prized, especially in Asian cultures, and foragers who have learned to identify this plant in the wild can make a decent day's wages. Mushrooms are often wild foraged rather than cultivated, and some gourmet mushrooms are always wild foraged.

Here, wild Maine blueberries are a cash crop for those who harvest them, although cultivated blueberries are also appreciated. In the south, there are certain plants that are harvested as a part of the community tradition, like pokeweed (*Phytolacca americana* also known commonly as poke salad), a spring green.

While some wild foods are familiar to some people, for most of us, the idea of eating something we found in the woods, growing in a local park or cut from a roadside ditch is just as unimaginable as eating opossum. As such, eating wild foods has become one of those fringe activities, something that the hippies or greenies or tree huggers or eco-freakos do. Normal people do not forage, and the result has been a complete loss of centuries of knowledge that our ancestors simply took for granted. The result has been that, without grocery stores, seed companies and willing farmers, we do not know what to eat. Because people simply do not know enough to trust that they will not eat something poisonous, they do not eat any of it at all, and these wonderful food sources simply go feral. There are far more plants that will do no harm than there are plants that are deadly, and there are a significant number that, if properly harvested (correct part of plant for the time of year the plant is harvested, for instance) and/or properly prepared, are wonderful, delicious, healthful foods. The aforementioned pokeweed, if allowed to mature, is inedible but as an early spring green, is considered a delicacy.

Interestingly, many of our most beloved cultivated plants have some parts that are toxic. Tomatoes are probably one of the most recognized foods in our culture. They are used in many of our favorite ethnic dishes from American-Italian cuisine to Tex-Mex fare. French fries would simply not be the same without tomato ketchup.

Speaking of French fries, another well-known and much loved food is the potato, the root of a plant from the same family as the tomato. Both plants are nightshades, and there are probably those reading who felt a shiver tingle down the spine at the mention of *deadly nightshade*, a mysterious, much feared flora. But people eat tomatoes and potatoes every day with no ill effects. In my house, potatoes are a staple. I grow them every year and store them over winter. They are a much loved food in our house because of their versatility. The potato can be baked, fried, scalloped, mashed, roasted, added to soups and stews or made into a soup all its own, dressed up and twice baked, made fancy in the French au gratin style and even grated and made into hash. Like most people, we know to eat the root, but not the aerial parts of the potato.

Although the well-loved tomato plant also has toxic leaves, we know to eat the fruit raw or cooked into a sauce for pizza, or ketchup for dipping French fries. Most folks would not even think of eating the poisonous leaves.

Rhubarb is another familiar plant that contains some toxic parts. The leaves contain oxalic acid, which is poisonous in large quantities. While small quantities, a leaf or two, will not kill us, it probably would not do us any good, either. The stems, which are the familiar rhubarb, are delicious and a spring treat in the northeast, especially baked in a pie with strawberries.

By contrast, we eschew some plants that can be consumed in their entirety, labeling them invasive or weeds, or some other derogatory term for an unwanted plant. In fact, one very well-known and much abhorred plant has become a garden nemesis, and poisons have been specifically formulated to rid our landscaped lives of this pest. Every part of this plant, *Taraxacum officinale*, commonly known as dandelion, can be eaten. In the spring, the early greens are wonderful, either eaten raw in a salad or sautéed with butter and garlic, especially after a winter-long diet of stored foods, devoid of anything fresh or green. Chopped and added to scrambled eggs, dandelions are a nutrient-packed treat. The flowers make delicious fritters when dipped in batter and fried, and they can also be steeped in water and made into wine. The roasted root, we have recently discovered, makes an amazing coffee-like beverage, and yes, it tastes very much like coffee, especially with a little cream and sugar.

Like most people, we had some trepidation about eating something that was simply growing where people walked, kids played and dogs ... well, you know ... did what dogs do in the grass. Until we started keeping our own garden, and realized that, while people do not usually just walk through the garden, the kids do not play in the beds, and we try to keep the dogs out, there are animals that do enter our garden space and do what animals do. Some animals eat the plants. Some do other things. We also use animal fertilizers in the garden, which is wholly organic and has never had any chemical fertilizer or pesticide treatments — not because we are all gung-ho about the organic ideologies, but because we have never wanted to spend the money on something that our rabbits and chickens provided for free. At some point, we made that tiny step outside of the notion that the food in the garden was somehow more pristine, more safe, than the food we found out in the woods.

We might understand (or even agree with) some of the rationale against foraging. Having foraged among curious stares of people in passing cars, we can understand why most folks would rather not open themselves to that sort of scrutiny. It is a little intimidating. We can also understand the ick-factor associated with plucking something having no idea what might have landed on the leaves we intend to eat, but when we start considering some of the reasons to forage, arguments against begin to pale. For us, the reasons to forage far out-paced any reasons not to.

While there will be people who argue that wild food has a greater potential to be deadly, over the years, we have come to believe this is not true. As Americans, we want to believe that the days of Upton Sinclair's *The Jungle* with its horror of slaughterhouse atrocities and unsanitary conditions are far, far behind us. We would love to believe that the formation of such oversight agencies as the FDA and the USDA, which are supposed to ensure that the food and medicine we buy will not kill us, means that our food supply is safe from food-borne contaminants. In a perfect world that would be true. We do not live in a perfect world.

According the Centers for Disease Control (CDC), food-borne illnesses cause about 128,000 hospitalizations and 3,000 deaths every year in the United States. Those numbers are bad enough, but when one considers that the CDC also estimates 48 million people fall sick due to food poisoning from contaminated food, being able to trust the safety of our food industry becomes a little more difficult.[1]

One of the first big recalls that comes to mind is the Jack in the Box tainted hamburger scandal in the early 1990s. Beef contaminated with E. coli bacteria made its way into the fast-food chain, where the hamburgers were, reportedly, not properly cooked. Four children died, and hundreds of people were sickened from eating the contaminated beef. Millions of pounds of beef were recalled.

The positive was that it forced the slaughterhouse in question to clean up its act.[2] The negative is that four children died and hundreds of people had to get sick before any corrective measures were taken. The question on many minds during that time, and that continues to plague us as parents, is why did four children have to die to make the food industry accountable for ensuring that our food supplies are safe?

Wouldn't it have been nice if it were a one-time incident? If the meat industry had looked at the recall of millions of pounds of beef and the loss of so many millions of dollars as their wake-up call?

Unfortunately, while it would seem that the food industry would have learned from that tragedy, the reverse actually seems to be true, and rather than being more careful, the industry, as a whole, has become more lax. Or maybe we have just become hypersensitive to the issue of food recalls.

Regardless, over the last two decades, the number of food-borne illnesses and deaths resulting from improperly or carelessly processed foods from our industrial food complex does not seem to be decreasing. In fact, it seems like every other day some new type of food is being recalled because it is contaminated.

In 2012 alone, several widely publicized recalls occurred, including a Nesquik recall (a chocolate-flavored drink mix powder favored by kids), a recall of several types of bagged salads from the Fresh

Express Company (that was implicated in 2010 for tainted spinach) and, most recently, another huge peanut butter recall (to follow the 2011 recall of several major brands, a result of contamination at their shared processing facility), which this time, also includes a brand sold at Trader Joe's. In our yuppie foodie fantasies, we could accept that Nesquik (which most food-conscious folk would never consume anyway) is being recalled, but to have spinach and anything from the iconic Trader Joe's recalled is unconscionable. If food from Trader Joe's is not safe, what is? we mutter.

The US economy loses $7 billion per year on food recalls.[3] If they can afford to lose that much money to tainted food, the profits for cutting corners and ignoring human health and safety must be enormous. There seems to be very little incentive to do better.

For us the choice between eating potentially deadly food from the industrial food complex or trusting that the food we find growing wild would be at least as safe was pretty much a no-brainer. The difference is that, with wild foods, we never assume that it is clean and sanitary, and because we do not know what it might have come in contact with, we handle it much more carefully. Most Americans assume that the food in the grocery store is grown and processed by someone whose livelihood depends on our willingness to buy that product. If we die from eating the food, they lose a customer and, thus, some of their potential profit. It would seem logical, therefore, that they would be very concerned about making sure their food does not kill anyone.

In a perfect world, right?

It is a constant surprise to witness the cavalier attitude that seems so prevalent in the industrial food complex when it comes to ensuring that they are doing their best to provide the most satisfactory product. Too often these days, a product substandard in every way except visual aesthetics seems to have become the norm rather than the exception.

Although it is bad enough that too much of our food makes us sick from bacterial contamination, in the past two decades, the news has been full of stories of other problems with our industrial food. One of the most talked about food issues these days, especially among people who are concerned about the long-term health effects of chemicals on our foods, is GMO (genetically modified organisms) or GE (genetically engineered) food crops.

Genetically engineered crops are not entirely new. Scientists first discovered the ability to transfer DNA characteristics from one organism to another in the 1940s, and the first genetically modified plant was a 1983 antibiotic-resistant tobacco plant. In 1994, a tomato that was genetically modified to give it a longer shelf life was introduced into the human food supply. In 1995, a handful of genetically modified plants were approved for commercial production, and by 2011, the US (a leader in the GM crop production) had twenty-five commercially approved GM products.[4]

At first, the public seemed either ambivalent or unconcerned about these crops, and of course, the biotech industry touted their product for its potential to make food last longer, to be more resistant to crop failures and to grow bigger or in smaller spaces. The rationalization from the biotech industry was that GMOs would be the cure for world hunger. With these amazing crops that were drought resistant or pest resistant or resistant to whatever other plant infirmities that could be corrected by splicing one unrelated organism into the seed, famine could be eradicated, and everyone could have a Big Mac (from beef raised in a confined animal feeding operation or CAFO) with a side order of fries.

When the shelf-stable GMO tomato started making the news, there was an immediate backlash from the organic eaters. The tomato was labeled a Frankenfood, and cartoons of a garish, sick-looking tomato and pictures of mutant people who consumed these Frankenfoods started popping up and caused a ripple of concern that would eventually turn into a global wave.

In 2000, the fact of GMOs in our food stream finally made the public consciousness. In September, a massive food recall of taco shells, manufactured by Kraft Foods, Inc., and sold in grocery stores under a license from Taco Bell, made the news. They had been made using Starlink corn, a GMO that had not (yet) been approved for human consumption. Even though there was no reported evidence of harm to its customers, Kraft Foods, Inc. decided to voluntarily recall the product, because the corn was not approved for human consumption. It was a $50 million mistake, a pittance for a company with $27 billion annual profit.

Unfortunately, even this very high-profile incident and Kraft Foods' unwillingness to experiment on their human customers with a product that had not been adequately tested did not stop the biotech industry from continuing its research and development of genetically engineered seeds. Today, more than a decade after Kraft Foods, Inc. did the noble thing and recalled a questionably safe product, the processed food industry has fully embraced the cheaper GMO option. In fact, Kraft is now using many GMOs or GMO ingredients. An estimated 80 percent of processed foods contain GMO ingredients,[5] the chief culprits being soy and corn.

Over 90 percent of the soy beans grown in the US are from GMO seed (although this appears to be changing, thanks to consumer efforts), and soy is a pervasive ingredient throughout the food industry, found in everything from baked goods to chewing gum. Ingredients like lecithin, monoglycerides, diglycerides and textured vegetable protein are often a soy-based product, and chances are better than not that it is grown from GMO seed.

Corn is often disguised in food labels under such names as dextrin, fructose, lactic acid, malt extract, maltodextrin, monoglycerides, pectin, sorbitol and hydrolyzed vegetable protein. It is also used in a variety of food preservation applications, like waxing and gassing to improve the aesthetics and/or prolong the shelf life of grocery store foods. Even if one is successful in avoiding processed foods that contain corn, if one eats CAFO meats, one will be exposed, as a secondary consumer, to GMOs, as GMO corn is the primary feed in concentrated animal feeding operations.

If it were not bad enough that so much food in the grocery store has been tainted with corn or soy, anything containing sugar could be GMO. Fifty-four percent of the sugar consumed in the US is from sugar beets, 90 percent of which are from GMO seed. Unless it specifically states it is sweetened with cane sugar, there is a very good chance that a product is sweetened with either GMO corn syrup or GMO sugar beets.

We like to think that, by eating foods that carry the organic label, we can avoid GMO products, but that may be a mistaken assumption, because corn derivatives are used, even in the organic industry, as preservatives, washes and waxes.

The biotech industry would like us to believe that their products are perfectly safe, and that splicing genes is no different than the centuries of hybridization and breeding that produced yellow roses and cold-hardy chickens. The fact is that breeding a chicken with a chicken to single out certain characteristics is significantly different from splicing a tomato gene with a gene from a salmon to give the tomato a longer shelf life.

We want to trust that while we work at transcribing audio recordings of medical reports into words on a page — or whatever we do *to make our living* — those people who are in charge of growing our food are being careful to ensure that our food is safe and healthy. That would be our mistake. For the companies responsible for developing the seeds to grow the majority of our crops, it is not about keeping us healthy. For them, it is about the money, and that is all.

When it comes to testing the safety of genetically modified organisms for use by humans, no one seems to want the responsibility of making sure the food being grown is okay to eat. In a *New York Times Magazine* article, "Playing God in the Garden," Philip Angell, the Director of Corporate Communications for Monsanto, is quoted as saying, *"Monsanto should not have to vouch for the safety of biotech food. Our interest is in selling as much of it as possible. Assuring its safety is the FDA's job."* The FDA's response to the testing of GMOs is documented in its publication "Statement of Policy: Foods Derived from New Plant Varieties" (GMO Policy), *"Ultimately, it is the food producer who is responsible for assuring safety."* [6]

In short, the company responsible for putting this food into our fields, and ultimately onto our plates, does not feel compelled to ensure that it is safe for humans, and neither does the taxpayer-funded department of the federal government whose job it is to oversee food safety.

For most, the lack of evidence is enough to ease their minds and believe that it might be okay. There is some good deal of truth in the cliché *ignorance is bliss* — while what we do not know can kill us, absent the knowledge of our impending demise, we can be blissfully happy in the moment.

Unfortunately, increasing research suggests that GMOs are not just not healthy but can significantly damage our bodies. At the same time that GMOs have become entrenched in our American diets, researchers around the world are discovering some long-term devastating health effects from continued exposure to GMO foods. A study by researchers in Russia found some startling results with hamsters fed a diet of GMO soy.[7] Similar research has resulted in countries worldwide rejecting not only GMO seeds, but also food imports from the US that might be GMO products.[8]

For more than two decades, Europe has had a ban on selling products with GMO ingredients. Russia has recently put a moratorium on the import of any potentially GMO foods from the US, and Peru has banned GMO seed entirely.

When faced with these facts, we have to wonder why our own government keeps approving the use of these products for human consumption.

As if GMOs were not bad enough, food packaging is a concern, in particular cans lined with the plastic Bisphenol-A (BPA), which was first synthesized by chemists in the late 1800s. Scientists have known since the 1930s that it had endocrine-disrupting properties. However, it was not until a 2007 investigative study by the *Milwaukee Journal Sentinel* that any risks associated with the use of BPA made the public consciousness. Since then, many more studies have seemed to support the notion that there are significant risks associated with the use of BPA in food containers.

Maine's governor, Paul LePage, found himself in a bit of hot water when he flippantly demanded to know what the problem with BPA was, except that women might "grow little beards." Unfortunately, the damage to our human bodies from endocrine-disruptive substances goes quite a bit further than simply producing facial hair on women.

A 2008 study conducted by researchers from the US and Canada using primates showed that BPA not only impacted reproductive health, but also affected brain function by disrupting memory and learning and increasing the incidence of depression.[9] One would think that knowing BPA affects a woman's reproductive health would be enough to ban the chemical, and if it is not, that knowing it could damage brain function would do the trick, but additional research has revealed some even more concerning effects. Researchers from the National Institute of Agronomic Research in Toulouse, France, found a link between BPA and intestinal damage.

Whoa!

For us, as parents with young children, concerns about potential reproductive cancers were enough. All of the other issues with BPA were just additional reasons to avoid the chemical when possible, and one more food item was jettisoned from our diet — anything that comes in a can.

Again, our choices seemed pretty clear. We could try to ignore any research that has shown the negative health consequences of relying on the industrial food complex to feed our family, or we could find alternatives. We decided to find alternatives.

The first option was to localize our diet. The food from our local farmers is less likely to contain hidden ingredients. For example, the apples straight from the pick-your-own (PYO) orchard are not likely to be waxed with a GMO corn-based wax. In fact, they are not waxed at all, and from the look and feel of the other produce available from my small local farmer, nothing is waxed or gassed. It is all fresh, never put into cans. The food is grown, often using organic techniques (no chemical fertilizers or pesticides), and then harvested and sold — sometimes on the same day. Several years ago, we visited a local winter farm store, and as we walked into the building, one of the people at the farm entered the back door, brushing snow off the kale, which she had just harvested. I bought a bunch.

We also grow some portion of our food, but living on an oddly shaped quarter of an acre suburban lot in a part of the country with a short growing season in a community where we were denied a permit to erect a solar-heated geodesic dome greenhouse, so that we could extend the season and/or grow food year-round, limits us.

And so we chose to also pursue the third alternative to trusting the industrial food complex, and that is to forage some portion of our diet.

People ask how I know that the food is safe, and their question is not how do I know that I can eat that plant, but rather how do I know that the plant has not been contaminated. The primary concern is with heavy metal contamination, specifically lead. Research has shown that lead contamination in plants, while it should be noted, is not as alarming as we have been encouraged to believe. The highest risk areas for lead contamination are close to building foundations (principally from lead-based paint dust) and near roads from auto exhaust,[10] which would seem to suggest that plants foraged in the fields, woods and parks near our suburban homes are probably okay.

The other comforting fact about metal absorption is that the fruiting parts of the plant are not likely to be contaminated at all.[11] Leafy green parts and roots are the concern, not that the plant itself is tainted, but rather, that there might be contaminates on the surface, i.e., dust on the leaves or polluted dirt on the root. A thorough washing will eliminate those contaminates.

That said, certain plants, considered to be filters, may absorb some environmental contaminates. We are careful about where we choose to harvest those plants. For instance, cattails are known to be filters, and so we would never harvest cattails that grow near a major highway.

Foraging was once a regular part of daily life. Before there was farming, there were the hunters and gatherers. A misconception about the daily toil of the hunter-gatherer versus the agrarian is that foraging for food requires a great deal more energy than farming. The reverse is, actually, true. The average peasant farmer worked from sun-up to sundown — just to put food on the table. Assuming an average of eight hours of sunlight, the average work week was fifty-six hours. By contrast, a hunter/gatherer — who knows what to look for — will spend about three hours per day looking for food and have the rest of the day free for doing whatever else takes his fancy. Three hours per day, seven days a week is twenty-one hours devoted to finding food.

Agrarian civilizations are only a few thousand years old and only became a regular way of life in North America when the Europeans landed. It is believed that the native populations, in the area where we live, were horticulturists. That is, that they grew some crops, but subsisted primarily on foods they foraged or hunted. If the genealogical research conducted by several family members is accurate, our hunter-gatherer lineage is as recent as 400 years ago — a countable number of generations back to a time when our kin lived completely off the land. Imagine. No grocery stores. No pre-packaged, GMO-tainted food items. No factory farms. No feedlots. Food was, mostly, what one could find, and contrary to common belief, hunter-gatherers were not half-starved barbarians who thanked their gods when the Europeans landed on their shores bringing with them their salted pork and dried peas. In his book *1491*, which discusses the Americas prior to the European colonization, Charles Mann states that journal entries from ships' captains claimed the so-called Indians were "strikingly healthy specimens." (p. 50). He estimates their daily caloric intake had been around 2,500 calories.[12]

When first learning to forage, we did not know a lot of those facts, but the more we learned about the food industry, the more important learning to identify wild foods became to us. Then, the more we started learning about the health benefits of wild foods, the idea of incorporating them into our diet became more appealing.

For us, it was a case of opening Pandora's box. What burst out at us when we first opened that lid was all the vile, unhealthy ugliness that is our money-centric corporate industrial food complex. Also, like Pandora, once we moved past the ugliness and beyond the fear, we found way down at the bottom of the box hope that we could escape most of the damage that has been done to our bodies and would be done to our children's bodies by changing not just our diet, but our mindset and accepting that nature does provide, if we are just willing to accept her gifts.

CHAPTER 9

Food Scarcity and the Increasing Costs of Food

W E HAVE NEVER, REALLY, BEEN HUNGRY. There have been times, as children in the 1970s recession with moves or life transitions that upset the flow of income, during our starving-student college days and early in our post-college careers, when sometimes the dollars did not stretch far enough to buy the exact food we wanted and also pay other mounting debts. There have been times when we had enough food to keep us going, but not enough to maintain our weight and the result was an unintentional twelve-pound weight loss. Even with those experiences, however, we have never been truly hungry in a too weak to move, gut-sucking, painful way.

This makes our whole fixation on food scarcity so bizarre and interesting. There is no experiential basis for us to be so concerned about our own hunger or the potential of our kids being hungry. It can, perhaps, be chalked up to a very vivid imagination, or maybe it was reading John Steinbeck followed by dozens of other novels, stories and movies set in times of scarcity, whether historical events post-apocalyptic tales. For whatever reason, the fear of starving has occasionally resulted in some odd behavior, like saving sauce packets from take-out restaurants for a Y2K soup.

There is a story about the ways people responded to hunger during the 1930s Depression. As it is told, some people would go into a restaurant and order a cup of tea, which was served as a cup of hot water with a tea bag on the side. When this arrived, the customer would pocket the tea bag for later, and then, dump tomato catsup, which was a free condiment on every restaurant table, into the hot water — instant tomato soup. Once, a few years before the Y2K scare started making headlines, we had some family visiting. We had gone to a local Mexican take-out joint. With a lot of people to feed and a very large order, we asked for extra salsa packets — just in case. The cashier eyed our order and asked us what kind — mild, medium or hot. We wanted an assortment, and what we ended up with was a whole mixed bag of salsa packets. We still had that bag when the news started reporting in earnest about the potential for worldwide disaster if a computer glitch that would disable all of the computers worldwide were not fixed. Word on the street was that as the clock ticked beyond the midnight mark on December 31, 1999, every computer would just stop, and the entire world economy, which is run by computers, would screech to a halt. In the days leading up to Y2K, we joked about our salsa packets being our Y2K food, but there was a touch of real concern there. If *they* were right and life as we know it did come to an abrupt end ... well, we had salsa soup — just add water.

Obviously Y2K passed without a ripple. The computers did not stop working. The world did not collapse.

Then, just over half a decade into the new millennium, we ended up on the Internet as bloggers and were introduced to the theory of peak oil. At that time, very few people even knew the term, had studied the work of M. King Hubbert (a geologist who first brought attention to the fact of our limited oil supply), understood what he had predicted and could see it playing out in the real world. According to peak oil theory, there is a finite amount of oil available in the ground, and the peak is when the amount of oil being used is equal to the amount being extracted. The peak is not when the oil runs out but rather when supply and demand are equal, and there is no way to increase supply.

It is like climbing Mt. Everest. The peak is the top, and those who get to the top struggle to get there. It takes a long time and a lot of work. They reach the top and have a party. And then, they have to go back down. The journey is not over at the peak, and neither is our access to oil.

The other thing about reaching the peak is that getting there took a long time, but coming down goes a lot faster — just like mountain climbing. Globally, the world is using as much oil as it is producing, but at the same time, as economies that have not been using much oil until now continue to get bigger, the demand for oil increases. Demand is growing, but worldwide production is decreasing, and we have a situation where we need or want more, but there simply is not more to have.

The US is still producing oil, but we import four times what we produce. As the demand continues to increase but the production does not, because we are taking as much out of the ground as fast as possible, the price of oil will continue to increase. The peak oil theory states that the cost of extracting oil will eventually exceed the profit to be made from selling it. At that point, either an alternative fuel will be found, or (more likely) we will simply learn to live without it.

The United States reached peak oil production in the 1970s. The North American continent is one of the most explored land masses on the planet. If there was oil to be found, US geologists found it. The US has been a net importer of oil for several decades. The estimated world peak oil production was around 2005.

When one first hears about peak oil, it is with some curiosity, but perhaps not a full understanding. We might think of peak oil as just resulting in higher prices at the gas pump, or those of us old enough to remember the 1970s energy crisis might envision rationing, long lines or even No Gas signs at the gas station. We might realize that limited availability may require us to make some lifestyle changes: sell our gas-guzzling pickup truck and buy a hybrid, learn some of those gas-saving driving techniques or limit and/or combine driving trips. We might also consider things like finding a job closer to home, negotiating a part-time telecommuting option or becoming a home-based entrepreneur so that we do not have to drive to work. Initially, our thoughts about how the oil crisis will personally affect us mainly have to do with operating our private vehicles, and we do not consider there is more to our oil dependence than gasoline for our cars.

Then, the proverbial light bulb goes off, and we start to understand the true implications of life without oil. We realize that, for the past hundred years, we have been building a society that is completely dependent on this oil and, more importantly, completely dependent on having unlimited cheap access. Everything we do, everything we eat, everything we wear, everything we need to simply survive is drenched in oil.

Here in the northeast, oil is the primary heat source in most homes, but even those who do not rely on heating oil are still somewhat dependent on oil for heat. Gasoline, to power those chainsaws or the cars used for moving the wood, is made from oil. Wood pellets require oil for their manufacture and transport. Even natural gas or propane is dependent on oil. Those very few who use electricity for heat (which is cost prohibitive in very cold climates) also depend on oil for mining and transporting coal, one of the primary fuels used in electricity generation.

Our food production industry uses oil in every single step of the process, from the chemicals that are used to make the plants grow bigger or produce more fruit, to the machines that are used in the planting and harvesting, to the facilities where the produce is refrigerated, to the trucks that transport food from storage warehouses to the stores where we buy the produce. Even the stores, themselves, are heavily drenched in oil from the lighting to the refrigeration. Most of the grocery stores we visit today, our so-called *super*markets, could not function without copious amounts of cheap oil.

And that's just raw plants. Processed foods take even more energy to get from raw ingredient to a box on the grocery store shelf — everything from the cooking of the products to the packaging need vast amounts of energy. Most of us have no idea how much, because both the food production industries and the oil industry here in the US are heavily subsidized by government money.

Without the availability of cheap energy, the price of food increases, and that is what has been happening. Over the past twelve years, the price of food commodities has steadily increased. According to the FAO food price index chart, the price index for all food commodities increased from 90 in 2000 to 213 as of August 2012. The price index for cereals more than tripled in that same time from 85 in 2000 to 260 as of August 2012.[1]

Part of the reason for these price increases has to do with the continuing creep upward in the price of oil (in 2008, the price of oil shot up to $140 per barrel and then plummeted to $40 per barrel, but the price has been steadily and slowly increasing since then. It was cautioned that the economy could not bear prices above $80 per barrel, which is where prices have pretty much remained for most of the last two years). Another reason is the devastating crop failures worldwide as a result of increasingly unsettled weather patterns, which scientists believe are being caused by an overall global climate change phenomenon that is, ironically enough, being blamed on the excessive use of fossil fuels.

In the breadbasket of the United States, a drought, the most severe since the 1930s Dust Bowl, has plagued farmers for the past several years. Flooding in Pakistan and Russia in 2011 destroyed whole fields. Freak frosts destroyed much of the orange crop in January 2012[2] in Florida and devastated commercial apple growers in the northeast in 2010. Early springs have negatively affected maple syrup producers in the northeast. Essentially, anywhere food is grown, which is pretty much everywhere, unusual weather patterns are destroying the crops — especially in the last decade.

The first to feel the effects are the farmers, of course, but as John Boyd, a farmer in Virginia, warns in an interview that appeared on NPR:

> It's a real troubling ... effect for — not just for farmers but for the consumers too. The consumers are going to see the high cost of food that shows up in the supermarket. The high cost of beef and poultry, because soybean and corn are used to feed these commodities. So it's going to be a real troubling effect for everybody.[3]

The weather anomaly is forcing farmers out of business, and those who survive will be the ones who have changed their business strategy to give them a niche market (like the farmer's market purveyors who have diversified their crops or those who transitioned to organic offerings) or the ones who did not allow themselves to incur too much debt as they built their farms.

As more farmers go out of business because of crop losses, and fewer farmers are growing what used to be grown by many, there is less food being grown, which leads to shortages. The law of supply and demand states that when the supply exceeds the demand the price will go down. The inverse is also true. If there is less corn available, the cost of buying corn increases, and any products made with corn (including, as Mr. Boyd points out, animals raised on corn feed) will cost more. The combination of crop failures coupled with fewer farmers, means that the cost of food will also increase, and as is evidenced by the food price index chart, this is proving true.

This is not even considering the possible implications of a disruption of the food supply chain to grocery stores. Granted, any break in this system will most likely be localized, but the effects would be devastating to those communities who find themselves unable to stock the grocery store shelves because of extreme weather. Recently, for instance, Hurricane Sandy passed through the eastern US and knocked out power to many areas for long periods of time. This included power to some food distribution warehouses, which were forced to refuse deliveries because they could not store the food products that arrived.

Here in southern Maine, one of our major grocery stores is Hannaford Bros, which started out as a local family-owned supermarket. They have over 180 stores and three distribution centers — two in Maine and one in New York. If each of the three distribution centers services an equal number of stores, and only one was knocked out, that would still be sixty stores that would be without supplies. If the emergency lasted for more than three days (the number of days for which the average store is stocked), it would be a devastating blow to our on-demand lifestyles.

As we became aware of the implications of peak oil, and we started paying attention to climate change, and the potential for a worldwide economic collapse became more plausible, the potential for a food scarcity event seemed not just likely but highly probable. Riots in the Middle East (Tunisia, Algeria and Egypt) in January 2011 were directly related to the increasing food prices and the inability for the average person to feed his/her family.[4] In Europe there have been similar strikes and protests related to food and oil prices.

From our very comfortable and well-fed position in suburban southern Maine, we watched these events unfold. We remain grateful for the bounty of our lives, but we have never taken the attitude that it could not happen to us.

Which is a good thing, because while much of the US has not experienced many of the extremes seen in other places, there is no arguing that, as a country, we have also been hit pretty hard by the economic downturn. Thousands of businesses, both big and small, shuttered in the last five years, leading to millions of jobs lost — jobs that may never be recovered. In the years following the great real estate market crash of 2008, the U-3 unemployment rate (unemployed workers who are actively searching for a new job, and usually calculated from those who are receiving unemployment benefits) soared to over 10 percent. There are a lot of problems with this number, including the fact that after a certain time period, whether or not those people become employed, they are no longer eligible for unemployment benefits, and cease to exist, statistically. The reported number does not account for all of those people who have been unemployed long enough to be discouraged about finding a job (U-4 rate) and those who are unemployed but are not really looking for a job, although they would be happy to have one (U-5 rate). No media-reported number counts those people who are underemployed, those who took jobs with significant pay cuts just to have a job but who have to make significant lifestyle changes to support themselves at the much reduced income level (which may include selling or losing one's home). This number is a little more sobering, soaring to over 16 percent.[5] Some pessimistically claim the number is higher.

Homelessness across the US increased significantly over the past four years. A Google search on "homelessness in the suburbs" yielded over six million related articles. According to a 2009 article in *USA Today*, the most disturbing trend in the increase in homelessness is the rising numbers of families and those in suburban and rural areas who are classified as homeless. As the article states, homelessness is no longer just an urban problem, and contrary to what we like to believe, the potential to find oneself homeless is no longer relegated to those who are drug-addled or mentally ill.[6] In short, it can happen to anyone. Without a home, weathering those tough situations like unemployment and hunger becomes even more difficult.

Equally concerning, and perhaps related, is the number of individuals and families being served by food pantries, and those who are seeking aid from government food subsidy programs like SNAP. By government reports, the use of food stamps has increased 46 percent.[7]

What matters to us is not which numbers are right or wrong. Regardless of the numbers, it is all pretty stark. Worse, though, is not what the media is reporting but what it is failing to report. We hear the talk on the streets, our friends and neighbors who relate their kinds of financial problems, how the increases in food and fuel prices are forcing them to make changes — some positive, some not so much. In spite of what our government and the media are telling us, the cost of feeding one's family continues to increase. That is not to say that there is not enough food, because the world produces an extraordinary amount, but more and more it is going to the person who can afford to pay the most. Right now that someone is those of us who were fortunate enough to be born in the West (North America, Europe, Australia). We are not so naïve as to believe that we will always be that someone, and there is as much a chance as not that our family could end up on the side of the fence where we cannot afford to buy what we need for sustenance.

We might be accused of being a tad pessimistic. In fact, that is not entirely true, because while we do believe that we could, at any moment, lose our incomes and end up destitute, we also believe in ourselves enough to be confident that our jobs are not our only source of support.

And that attitude is, ultimately, what led us to our current lifestyle. Seeing what was happening, we decided to not allow circumstance to force us into a situation where we might have to make that very difficult decision between feeding ourselves and having a place to live.

At first, our response to a potential income loss was to attempt to become as self-sufficient as possible. We (principally, Wendy) felt we needed to grow our own food so that we would not be victims of the fluctuations in food prices, to limit our dependence on electricity and/or other fuels we could not find or produce ourselves and to develop a skillset that would enable us to provide for most of our daily needs, including making soap, sewing/knitting, wood carving, cooking and brewing. Our rationale was that if we could do it, we would not have to pay someone else to, and then we would not need as much money to survive.

We realized, though, that we were limited by our environment. Even with our limited skill and knowledge, we can grow an extraordinary amount of food on a quarter acre. Much of our onsite edible landscape is still new. For example, we have not yet had a first real harvest of apples, but we have not had to buy berries in a couple of years, because the black raspberry brambles are pretty generous. We have not bought eggs in six years, and our flock has increased from three hens to ten (both chicken and duck). We also raise between forty and fifty meat chickens each year — enough for one chicken approximately every week, with each providing three meals.

Unfortunately, raising as much food as we do, we still have not succeeded in supplying all of the dietary and caloric needs for our family, and with the increasing prices at the grocery store, we knew we needed to find another food source. The logical choice seemed to be learning to use what nature provided for free, for those with enough sight to see the plants as food and not just green stuff in the landscape.

With a combination of what we grow and forage (including hunting and fishing), we are pretty confident that we can feed ourselves and our children … come what may.

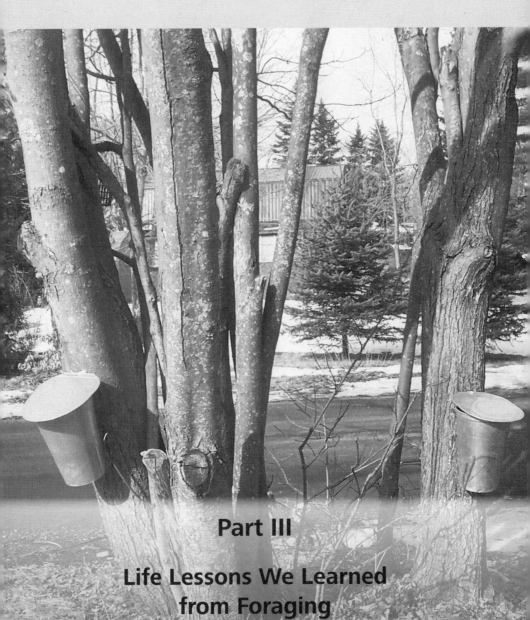

Part III

Life Lessons We Learned
from Foraging

CHAPTER 10

Procrastination Leads to Failure

*Only put off until tomorrow what you are willing
to die having left undone.*

— Pablo Picasso

Several years ago, we became acquainted with a home-schooling mom who explained that one of the many languages spoken in Africa had a word that describes that exact moment, often unremarkable to us regular, disconnected humans, when the season changes. The word is *kyah* (pronounced ki'ə). Her explanation was particularly insightful and clever, because it was the name of her first child — the *kyah* being that moment when she and her husband went from being a couple to being a family.

We are lucky to have four very distinct seasons in our temperate zone. We would have a hard time, if asked, to pinpoint our *kyah*, because there never seems to be that one exact moment when the season changes. For instance, snow means winter, but sometimes, when it seems like spring has fully arrived in Maine, we will still have more snow. Often we will say that the spring *kyah* is when the first robins appear, returned from their winter vacation in the south, but even that may not be completely accurate. There have been a lot of spring-like happenings before we see the robins, and there have been a few times when we have seen them in the snow.

More likely, there is not a single *kyah*, but many — many moments of transition, when one plant, particular to a time of year, pokes its head through the dirt and begins its journey through the warming and lengthening days, until months later the cycle is completed as the frigid winds and icy precipitation send it back into dormancy, until the cycle is renewed at the next spring *kyah*. Sometimes plants growing right next to each other will progress at different rates, and so even in that, there is no single transition, but many, even within the same species.

On a sunny early spring day, we decided to head out through the woods to a lovely field. It is a nice walk. Sometimes we take the dog out, too. He is happy to accompany us.

The wide path snaked through the woods, a mix of pines and hardwoods (like our beloved maples and oaks) growing close together, creating a deep shade even at this time of year when the deciduous trees had not yet begun to don their summer garb. During the summer, heading into the woods on any day above 80° is a welcome relief for us Mainers, for whom such temperatures can only be described as blistering. This day, though, in spite of the bright blue sky we could see peeking through the skeletal branches, in the dabbled shade of the dense forest, it was a bit chilly. We strolled along the path, occasionally stopping to visually mark the location of a plant that we knew would mature later into something we might want to use, but not tarrying long on our journey through the woods to our destination.

The end of the path is almost always a surprise. We know it is coming, but with the way the trees grow so thick on either side right where the woods give way to the clearing, it is not obvious that it is there. It is not like leaving a tunnel, the exit often visible as a tiny pinhole of light from journey's beginning growing bigger at the end.

Rather it really is like … well, a *kyah*, a sudden moment when the forest becomes a glade.

And there we were, walking out into a field, much of which was still brown. Little green blades of grass pushed up through the thatch of last year's crop that lay limp on the ground. The dead stalks of last year's Japanese knotweed stood broken and bent from winter's onslaught. On the other side of the field was one of two major roads that lead into our town. This time of year the traffic was sporadic and light.

In the very early days of spring, there is not a lot that we are familiar with. We know we could harvest burdock root, if we could identify the dead leaves. If we get it early enough, before the roots start putting energy into growing the plants, we could harvest wild carrot, Jerusalem artichoke (not something we have ever found wild, but it would be quite an awesome find) and dandelion root.

Timing is key, and in our on-demand culture, it is probably the most difficult habit to overcome — the propensity to believe that if we want it, we just need to go out and get it. Unfortunately (and really unfortunately for us, because we fell victim to our own failure to heed this fact too many times), nature simply does not work that way. There is food, and it is abundant, but it is like the proverbial smoke on the water, fleeting and temporary. As Janis Joplin proclaims in one of her songs, when it comes to foraging, especially, you have to "get it while you can." One day too late, and the roots are soft and mushy, the stalks are too woody, the fruits are too ripe.

What we experienced, because we failed, again and again, to actually learn the lesson, was that we could not wait until we were ready to go out and harvest. We needed to be available when the plants were ready to be harvested.

With a plan to forage as much as we could and to really incorporate foraged foods into our diet, rather than just our usual haphazard, opportunistic harvesting when out for a walk, the first day we ventured out to search for spring greens, we hoped to find some particular plants. We were looking for Japanese knotweed, dandelion greens and nettles — if we got lucky.

The knotweed was not quite ready. The little tops were crowning but had not grown enough for us to harvest any. The stalks need to be shorter than six inches, but at least tall enough to snip. These were not even close. We thought, maybe the next week we could get some. Likewise, the field was pretty well devoid of any dandelion flowers, although we did manage to snip a few leaves. The nettles were ready, and some of those came home with us.

The next week, we ventured out again to the same spot. In only seven days, the Japanese knotweed had grown tall enough to harvest. Some of the plants were so tall we could no longer eat them.

The dandelion flowers were also ready to be picked, and we brought home a small basket full of flowers, Japanese knotweed stalks and nettles. It was a good harvest. The next week, we had another good harvest, mostly of the same stuff.

As should not happen, but does too often to us modern humans, we focused our attention on the ridiculousness of modern life, and our quest for real, completely natural and healthy food was put on hold (and yes, the irony of the fact that people suffer from so many diet-related diseases, many that a more natural diet, like foraging provides, could cure, but that we do not make time for this organic way of life, does not escape me). By the time we returned, about six weeks after our first visit to the field, the Japanese knotweed stalks were all past harvest, and it was too early to consider taking the roots. The dandelion flowers were all gone to seed, and the leaves, which are best before the flowers bloom, were at that bitter stage where most people do not bother. The dandelion roots, like many roots in the late spring and summer, would need to finish out the cycle and would be best left until fall to harvest.

The worst discovery was the nettles, which had been decimated by the Red Admiral butterflies. We never faulted the butterflies for destroying the whole stand, hoping that the plants would be hardy enough to bounce back from the predatory onslaught, but it was tough to realize that our special patch of this amazing green was no longer available to us. It reminded us that waiting until we were ready often means that we do not get any.

In the foraging game, the life cycle continues to turn whether we make ourselves part of it or not. Humans have removed ourselves from the cycle and have become dependent on our agrarian culture, but even in that, crops fail, and sometimes the things we want at the grocery store are not there, either.

We still have not completely learned the lesson about procrastinating, but we did improve as we progressed through the summer. We made it a point, for instance, to visit the blackberries several times, before the season ended, and we were very conscious of the season changing from summer to fall, watching for when the acorns fell or when the apples were ready to be harvested.

Fortunately for us, our modern lives, though an impediment to timely learning, provide something of a failsafe that our ancestors did not have with their hunting and gathering. We still have the ability to fall back on all of the conveniences that exist in our culture. We can still go to the grocery store and fill our shelves with foods to sustain us when we get too busy to seek out the wisdom of the natural world. Our ancestors would have starved, or at least have led very difficult lives, had they fallen prey to our blunder. Interestingly, it is this safety net that both saves us and keeps us firmly anchored in the sadly disconnected, mostly dissatisfying, way of life that so many of us lead.

Perhaps, in some ways, we went through our own *kyah* as foragers. Still far from experts, we are comfortable with only a few plants that we really know how to use and enjoy eating, but we took that first very important step, which is changing our mindset from one in which foraging is just about finding trail food — if done at all — to an understanding that finding food in the wild is the way nature intended for us humans — all creatures, really — to eat. We cannot pinpoint the moment, that *kyah*, when we transitioned, but now that the season has changed, now that we have changed, there is no going back to where we were. We must continue the cycle. We have found that the way has been blazed by many who came before us, and eating wild foods is not some new, exciting adventure humans have just discovered, as much as it is a recapturing of who we really are.

Chapter 11

Success Means Paying Attention

The simple act of paying attention
can take you a long way.

— Keanu Reeves

FOR THE FIRST TIME, since we bought our house here in the suburbs fifteen years ago, we saw turkeys in our yard. We have
known for a very long time that they lived in the woods, leaving
their tracks in the early spring in patches of snow that had not yet
melted. Sometimes we would see signs of where they had roosted
in pine trees. Occasionally we would see them down the road at the
neighbor's house. We had a lot of theories about why they never
came up as far as our house — maybe because of our dogs, or perhaps because of our proximity to the main road with very busy and
fast traffic. Whatever the reason for their reluctance to wander up
here in previous years, they decided that it was not so important to
avoid this part of the road this year.

We had noticed that the rafter of turkeys was pretty big, between
eleven and twenty every time we saw them. While we do not know
the average size of a turkey rafter, this one seemed particularly large

for a flock of non-migrating birds with such a big stature. At some point during the summer or fall, we found an article that gave us a possible reason for how this particular gang could have grown so large.

If we travel back in time to the early spring of 2011, we were hosting a survival skills class for home-schoolers. Our teacher took us into the woods, where we spent hours learning and playing, both at the same time. One day, we were in a run-off ditch learning the difference between cattail and marsh grass, and our teenaged daughter looked down and noticed ticks crawling on her boots. Ticks. Yes, plural.

Ticks are a significant health concern in our area — they have been for many years. It is not new. In fact, the dreaded Lyme disease was named after a Connecticut town where it was first discovered in 1975.

Being aware of this fact, we are usually very careful to do a "tick check" when coming in from walking in the woods. We are very diligent about treating our pets so that they do not carry ticks inside the house on their fur. In spite of our care, however, we will usually find a few ticks on us, and those ticks go into a jar of alcohol, which we have dubbed "the tick jar." Our girls automatically find the tick-off tool and the tick jar when they find one of the little hitchhikers on them or our pets. Generally, however, unless we go in the woods, we do not have a lot of ticks.

In the spring of 2011, even just playing in the yard, the girls would come in with ticks on them, and never, in my whole life, have I been standing and seen ticks, not *tick*, crawling off the grass and onto my body.

Four years ago, in 2008, it was a banner year for acorns. There were so many that a friend, who lives on an even smaller lot and has only three oak trees shading her property, filled a thirty-gallon trash can with acorns — filled the can from the dropped nuts of only those few trees.

If one begins to connect dots, a very clear picture of cause and effect begins to emerge. Where there is a surplus of food, the population that eats that food explodes. Mice eat acorns. The year we had a surplus of acorns, here in our house, we had no mice — at least none that we saw or that our cat caught. With a surplus of food out in the woods, they had no need to come into our house.

The favorite food for ticks is mice, at least according to the article that we read. Mice eat acorns, and the population explodes. The ticks, with a much larger food supply, experience a population explosion as well.

In 2012, the ticks were not nearly as bad as the previous year, and we would have expected otherwise, that our incredibly mild winter would have allowed a greater number of ticks to survive. The fact is that the ticks may have survived the winter in mass quantities, which helped to ensure the proliferation of another species that preys on them — namely turkeys, and for the first time in fifteen years, we saw a flock of turkeys like nothing we had ever seen before.

Observing and being able to predict trends like that one are very valuable to a forager. Back during the year that we had such a huge acorn crop, we might not have been able to put together all of the particular pieces of the puzzle, but this year was a pretty good acorn crop, which means we might want to be a little extra careful during the tick season of 2014.

It is also likely that the oak trees will not be as generous again next year. Plants growing in the wild are never as predictable as what we find in the grocery store. When we want to serve asparagus wrapped in phyllo dough as an appetizer for the guests at our holiday parties, it does not matter that fresh asparagus is a spring delicacy in the northeast and is not growing fresh in December. As the drinking song says, "It's 5:00 somewhere." In our on-demand world, it is spring somewhere and someone is growing and harvesting asparagus and shipping it to our grocery stores here in Maine.

We have found that nature is never generous in quite the same way. There is always plenty of food to find, but perhaps not exactly the food we were looking for.

In the fall of 2011, when we first started harvesting wild foods with the intent of incorporating them into our regular diet, the food that gave us our start was apples, and that year, the wild apples were everywhere we looked. In fact, driving down the road, we spied apple trees, full to drooping, all over the place.

Then, when the 2012 apple season arrived, we went looking for apples and found only a few very small, gnarly-looking wild apples. It was a complete 180-degree turn from our previous year's experience.

Local apple growers seemed to have a good year, although news from other parts of the country, in particular Michigan, where reports stated that a mild winter followed by a late April frost devastated the apple crop, corroborating what we were seeing with the wild apples. Perhaps commercial growers have some way of protecting their blossoms that wild apples do not have, but whatever the case, the wild apple harvest was disappointing.

By contrast, everywhere we looked, we found berries. Our freezer was filled with all of the wonderful berries our bramble at home provided, and we were also gifted with wild blackberries and blueberries — more than enough to enjoy fresh and to store away for winter.

We were grateful for the berries, to be sure, but what we had hoped for was to have a good apple crop so that we could store a few gallons of wild apple wine. The few shriveled and bitter apples were hardly worth the effort of climbing into the trees to get the ones out of our reach, because not only were the trees sparse, but the apples were up in the top-most branches.

The lesson was that we could never become too dependent on one food or another. If the only food we knew to eat had been apples, we would have been very hungry, indeed. The lesson is applicable across the spectrum of wild foods that we enjoy, and we have not yet figured out how to predict what plant foods will do well and what will do poorly. The more we know, however, and the closer attention we pay to what is happening around us, the better we get at figuring out those little nuances that will tell us what to expect.

Paying attention to the signs served us well when it came time for our maple syrup harvest in the spring of 2012. It had been a particularly warm winter with very little snow. By the end of January, the snow was receding, and the daily temperatures were warming up significantly. We are accustomed to, and aware of, the phenomenon dubbed "January thaw" where the temperatures become spring-like for a few days to a week or two. It is always a nice, usually brief, reprieve from winter, and we enjoy the sunshine and warmer temperatures. This particular year, the significant difference was that the trees appeared to be coming alive.

Traditionally, maple sugaring season begins in mid-February and ends in mid-April. Toward the end of the run, many farms in our area will participate in Maine Maple Sunday, when they will open their farms to the public and serve a breakfast featuring the maple's gift. Maine Maple Sunday is typically the last Sunday in March, which is usually about when the season is beginning to wind down, the maple trees are starting to bud, and we know that spring has arrived.

Paying attention to the weather and watching the trees, we noted that things looked very different. We are not expert sugarers, by any stretch of the imagination, but this time, we decided to listen to that little voice, and we took a chance and tapped the trees, even though conventional wisdom would have advised us to wait a few more weeks, until February, at least.

Sure enough, the sap was flowing, and we were thankful for starting as early as we did. In order for the sap to flow, the daytime temperatures need to be in the upper 30s to mid-40s, and the nighttime temperatures have to be below freezing. If it is too cold or too hot, the sap will not flow. In 2012, the sugaring season in Maine was a very short four weeks, and by the beginning of March, the sap was no longer freely flowing, as most nighttime temperatures were staying well above freezing.

We have fifteen taps, and because we started early, we ended up with three gallons of syrup. Many home sugarers were not so fortunate, and we heard from many of our friends who tapped a week or two after we did and had a disappointing season.

With our limited number of taps, we must also be careful to select the best trees. In our early years of sugaring, we wasted some effort tapping the wrong trees. In fact, even occasionally tapping the wrong kind of trees. Without leaves, maple and oak trees are very similar, unless one looks more closely.

We have had friends ask how to identify maples in the early spring. After one has a bit of experience, and has developed the ability to pay attention to subtle details, it becomes much easier to discern an oak from a maple. Really, the trees give us a lot of clues. Looking up into the branches in the late winter or early spring, before buds appear, one might notice that some leaves may still be clinging to the mostly bare branches. That is a pretty big clue. Oak trees tend to hold their leaves; maple trees do not. Or, consider that the maples trees bud much earlier than the oaks. When it is time to tap, the maples will have tiny little buds, and the tips of the small branches will look red and alive. Buds on oaks grow in an alternate pattern, and those of the maples are opposite. Maple branches grow upward in graceful curves, but oak branches are crooked and gnarly. Paying attention ensured that we had a more bountiful harvest.

The maples have given us other clues. One year we noticed that some of our taps seemed to be flowing really well, where others were not doing so great. The best ones were in trees where the snow had melted from the base. We surmised that, with the snow cover gone, the sun was able to warm the soil around the roots and the sap flowed up better.

As with the maples, other plants will provide clues about how the season is progressing. Plants instinctively flower when the weather is right, independent of the calendar. Knowing that the flowers grew three weeks earlier than last year, a forager can reasonably predict an earlier harvest, providing more opportunity to watch for the edible parts to be ripe for picking. As we watched the season pass, we kept track of the timing of the plants. The maple season was about three weeks early. We continued to watch the development of the other plants, and through the entire summer and into fall, everything was two to three weeks early.

Making note of what we see happening in the world outside our windows has served us very well on so many occasions, and sometimes it is our car windows that we see out of.

During the last year, we coined a phrase to describe this habit we have of identifying edible plants while whizzing by the landscape at inhumanly fast speeds. The very first time we engaged in the practice was while were searching for chaga, although the dizzying effect of trying to peer closely at the birches and see the black scar of the chaga mushroom growing on the distinctive white trunks resulted in a bit of car sickness.

Over time we either got better at it, or we learned to start looking for things that do not require such close scrutiny (we never have positively identified chaga while speeding by in a car). Many of the wild apple trees we harvested in the fall were identified in passing. Many other plants are easy to identify (and return for later) while driving past, like milkweed and white pine.

Our favorite find, while practicing what we dubbed *high-speed foraging* was the blueberries we harvested in the industrial park. The general area had been scouted on foot (inadvertently), but when we went back, we were in a car, and identified the ripe berries while traveling at 25 mph. They were huge, and the bushes were completely full of the ripe fruits. Even going this fast, we could clearly see the deep blue-purple berries contrasted against the bright green leaves, and we picked more than five pounds on our first blueberry foray in the area. We returned some days later and gathered another five pounds or so from trees further down the road, and when getting out of the car to harvest the taller berry bushes, we also found some low-bush blueberries and picked from them as well.

We have learned how important it is to pay attention, because nothing will ever be exactly the same from one year to the next. Nature is no different than we are or than our home gardens are. We change, sometimes significantly, from day to day and year to year. My garden is always different, even though I often plant the same sorts of plants year after year.

This is also true of wild foods — they do not always grow the same way. If we become too complacent or unwilling to pay attention to the signs, we will have a very tough time making foraging a productive pastime. There are incredible benefits to foraging, and not taking advantage of those gifts, because we failed to pay attention, would be a shame.

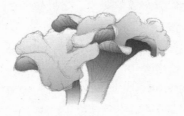

CHAPTER 12

Rule of Thirds for Foragers

I N THE 1930S, THE FIRST ALL-YOU-CAN-EAT BUFFET RESTAURANT opened in Minneapolis, Minnesota. These can be particularly problematic for little kids, whose eyes tend to be much larger than their stomachs, and as such, there is probably a lot more waste than is necessary.

As kids, we went on several occasions to our favorite all-you-can-eat buffet restaurant. The word "smorgasbord" was in the name of the restaurant. It would be many years before the real meaning of that word was truly understood. For kids, it just meant a lot of scrumptious choices with no restrictions on what food to put on our plates. It was worse than a candy store.

A sign posted at intervals on the sneeze guard above the warming tables warned those with big eyes and teeny-tiny tummies: "Take all you want, but eat all you take." Like most kids, we usually failed to comply.

As an adult, it has become much easier to put on the plate only what I can reasonably consume in one sitting. The lesson has been learned and heeded, but it was, ultimately, a lesson learned through activities like foraging.

Interestingly, since most of us do not forage, it is not something that most of us are able (or, perhaps, willing) to do, and we find ourselves in a society of people who have a strong tendency toward believing they need more than is actually necessary. The world is very much full of little big eyes.

Last year, we were invited to submit an application to a cable television show that depicts people, like us, who are not completely convinced that all is well in Oz. We are people who do not believe that the Wizard can (or is even willing to) try to find solutions to make things better — maybe even if our idea of better just means going back to whatever good life we believed is now slipping from our grasp. Many of the people who are featured on the show are pretty sure that the Wizard is corrupt, has tasted too much power and is bent on destroying not just the American way of life, but the world. For the record, the "Wizard" is not just one person but whoever is making the rules at the time. The Wizard is not a "he" or a "she," but a "they."

"Can you take some pictures of your storage areas?"

Clearly the show's producers were accustomed to people who live a bit differently than we do, and we had to think about this request. Should it be a picture of the shelves holding jars of home-canned goodness from our local harvest, the contents and quantity of which varies depending on the time of year? Should we take some pictures of the squash and potatoes we raised during the summer and had stored on the floor in our bedroom closet? Should we take pictures of the eggs … or rather the potential eggs that are stored in the chickens outside in the backyard?

We realized pretty quickly that we might have a problem with their request, namely, we are not the normal sort of preppers. If their cameras came at the wrong time of year, for instance, in April, there may be very little to see. We could photograph what we had, but we eat what we have stored, and by April our shelves are just not as full as they are in September, as most of it is eaten up. They will not be restocked until we start canning, sometime in June when the berries start getting harvested.

We do not have a hidden corner that is devoted to storing all of the goods that we have scored on sale or with our extreme couponing. There is no extra room in our house nor a wall of shelves in the garage or basement filled with dozens of containers of Secret® Baby-Powdered scented roll-on; cases of two-ply toilet paper; mint-flavored, fluoride toothpaste and Herbal Essence shampoo with enough canned tuna, boxes of Kraft Macaroni and Cheese and Chef Boyardee® raviolis to last our family of five for a full year. Mind you, we are not making fun of people who have these things. Preparedness is smart. We just approach it from a different angle.

We do not buy deodorant, for instance. Not ever. Having a shelf full of Secret® Baby-Powder scented roll-on would not make much sense for us. Even if we thought it might make a useful barter item in the event of a collapse, we just do not see much value in wasting our money on that very remote possibility.

While we do not use Secret®, we do use deodorant that we make ourselves, and we store the ingredients rather than the products. Unfortunately, a shelf with a couple boxes of baking soda and cornstarch, a jar or two of coconut oil and some vials of essential oils just does not have the same visual impact as the rows and rows of colorful store-bought products.

Likewise, we do not buy canned foods. Not ever. Instead of canned beans, we buy (or grow) dried beans and cook them ourselves. We grow and can our own tomatoes, peaches and applesauce. Peas are eaten fresh, in season, and occasionally frozen, and many of the other canned vegetables people buy are eaten fresh in season, frozen or home canned. We do not eat commercially canned vegetables now, and so it does not make sense for us to buy cans of food, even the dented, at bargain-basement prices. So, instead of beautifully organized shelves of symmetrical store-bought cans, we have several shelves of jars of food we harvest from our garden or that we bought in bulk and in season and preserved. In an average year, we will can over 100 jars of homemade goodness, including tomatoes, pickles, applesauce, peaches and strawberry preserves. We have also canned more difficult things like corn and meat, which require a bit of extra care and more than a simple water bath. Our shelves of canned goodness may produce prickles of envy from other canners, but we were given the feeling that most folks would not be particularly impressed — either with the amount of work involved in getting all of that food into all of those jars or with the incredible amount of food those few jars represent.

We also have a closetful of root-cellared vegetables, like potatoes and squashes, and our homebrew. Three or four dozen heads of garlic from our garden hang in the kitchen. Our freezer is full of the chickens we raised, and the cow-share and pig-share we bought.

The difference between our stored stuff and the stuff that makes for good television is that ours is perceived as being more perishable than what those who are featured on those programs store. The common belief among the general public seems to be that store-bought food will last longer, which probably is not true. While some might be perfectly content to eat store-bought pork-n-beans from 1999, very few people would be comfortable eating home-canned strawberry jam made that same year — even though the latter is probably a good deal safer and a whole lot healthier.

The television program producers needed more than we were able to show them, as our set-up must have appeared, in pictures, to be a very amateurish attempt at preparedness. What we know, however, that could not be conveyed in our photographs is it is not necessary to store everything. Mother Nature is incredibly generous, and very forgiving; all that we need can be found, if we are just willing to step outside and look for it.

So, we did not end up on the show, because we decided not to stress over whether our storage was acceptable. We surmised, given the kinds of things they seemed to want pictures of and our inability to produce a more substantial image, that our little suburban home-stead was not something the show's audience would find interesting. But the experience was a really good reminder for us of some basic human tendencies. In particular, the tendency in all of us to be hoarders.

Although most present-day Westerners have never experienced true hunger, let alone real famine, it is always in the back of our minds how easily it could happen to us. The pre-colonial era in Europe is depicted as one of deprivation and eking out an existence, and any-one with a standard public education was regaled with images and stories of the worldwide Great Depression during the 1930s. Those of us who were born during the Vietnam War Era recall the stark images of famine in Ethiopia. Those who have not negatively impacted by the economic downturn have some, perhaps more real, concerns, like weather-related crop failures, food riots and rising food costs, which only serve to increase our worry. These have resulted in a great temptation to succumb to our fear of going hungry and take all that we can get, storing it *just in case*.

The fact is that the potential for famine is ingrained in our agrar-ian culture. In the Judeo-Christian culture, this is an oft-discussed topic, starting at the very beginning with Joseph in Genesis, who won the Egyptian pharaoh's favor by warning of a seven-year famine and proved his worthiness to be remembered through history as a Prophet. Famine is very much a part of agrarian societies because crops fail, and when one is dependent on a particular food crop for sustenance, failure is inevitable.

Life, for foragers, can be more secure for the simple fact that they understand crop failures happen. Thus, we learn not to depend wholly on one type of food, because we recognize all sorts of vari-ables, that we cannot control, will affect how well a particular plant or animal grows.

For example, what might be to us minor fluctuations in tempera-ture can ruin an entire years' worth of maple syrup. When the buds start to form leaves, usually when the nights start to get above freezing, the sugaring season is over. We have had years where the season was two months long, and other years when it was three weeks. Since we cannot control the weather, and there is simply no chemical we know of that can make the trees produce better in spite of the weather, if we were wholly dependent on maple syrup, we would be in trouble.

It goes further though. It is not just that the weather will affect how well that plant produces, but that we can cause problems if we are too dependent on that one plant. Remember that we all have a tendency to want to take as much as we can get, but doing so as a forager could be devastating.

When tapping trees, for instance, it is important to pay attention to the size of the tree. While the sap from any maple can be made into syrup, tapping a too young tree, or putting too many taps into a larger tree can kill the tree. Dead trees do not give sap.

There is a beautiful land trust area where we have enjoyed the generous bounty of Mother Nature. Here we have found the most amazing crop of milkweed that we have ever seen. This is a wonderful and versatile plant, because so much of it is edible. Early in the season, the shoots are delicious as an asparagus-like vegetable. Later in the season, the buds are delicious chopped and added to quiche. The flowers can be battered and fried, and the pods can be steamed and eaten like green beans, or stuffed, like pasta shells.

Imagine, though, that some forager, giving in to the very human tendency to hoard, harvested every single early milkweed shoot that was available in this vast field? It would be a lovely treat for that one person for the entire year — milkweed shoots, like asparagus, can be blanched and frozen for use later. But what about everyone else? And here, we are not talking about other human foragers, who would surely be disappointed, too, but about the other creatures who depend on the milkweed? In particular, Monarch butterflies, who are already being devastated by habitat loss, would suffer.

In addition, if we were to harvest all of the milkweed shoots at the beginning of the season, we would eliminate the possibility of all the other wonderful ways to enjoy the plant. If there are no shoots, there will be no buds, no flowers and no pods.

When we forage, we follow — without fail — the Forager's Rule of Thirds:

1. Take one-third.
2. Leave one-third for others.
3. Leave one-third for the future.

When taking up to a third of the plants, we try to help the remainder to become healthier. We can do this not by razing the closest third available, but by selectively picking small plants that are being shaded or crowded out by other bigger plants. In helping to thin the plants out, we pick ones that do not appear as vigorous as those nearby but are still edible. This is similar to the native philosophy of hunting the old, least hardy-looking or weaker animals to keep the herd strong and virile.

Leaving one-third for others, including other species, provides for biodiversity in a given area. If we were to harvest all of the fruits from a particular stand of blueberries, for instance, some birds and animals, finding no food, would move to other areas to seek out a means to feed themselves. These species that have had to find food elsewhere may have provided something to the other local species, and without those animals, other dependent species may suffer. In the most extreme case, taking too much could cause an imbalance that threatens the entire ecosystem, including the plant that we came to harvest in the first place. At very least, it is simple courtesy to leave some behind for others to find.

The final third, or more, we leave to grow bigger and stronger to reproduce. If we fail here, there may be a much smaller offering, or no crop at all, in subsequent years. This vital part is the breeding stock for all future generations of that plant, or animal, species. If we devastate the entire population in this spot, at best we will have to find another place to harvest this food.

If enough people do this in enough places, we risk running species into extinction. We have seen this type of over-harvesting and hunting within the last hundred years or so. In the early 1900s, both whitetail deer and wild turkeys had been hunted nearly to oblivion in North America, because we as a culture did not follow these rules. Thankfully, we were able to reverse this, and populations have rebounded.

Depending on the plant, sometimes we do not even take a third at a time. We will often only take what we can reasonably use for one or two meals. We will eat one meal and preserve a second with the intention of returning for more later. Using the milkweed as an example, we might take only a shallow basketful of the early shoots. When the milkweed starts to bud, we might take a few from several plants, but always leave some on *each* plant, never harvesting one entirely.

If it is not a good year for that plant, that is if the plant does not seem to be growing very well, then we will take none at all. The lovely thing about foraging is that there are always alternatives. Unlike the grocery store, where the sale item is one choice for that price, in nature, there are usually plenty of options, and all of them are free. Perhaps not an exact one-for-one trade (like we may not get an asparagus-like plant if we cannot have milkweed), but in nature, there is a veritable smorgasbord of options.

CHAPTER 13

Know What Grows Where

WHAT WE DO NOT KNOW ABOUT GARDENING COULD — and does — fill volumes. What we know about gardening could be contained in a short article. It is not a case of having a black thumb, because we actually do have a pretty nice garden year after year, not without some small effort and attention on our part. Some of the best producers in the garden every year, however, are not things we intended to grow, but rather plants that volunteer and are allowed to grow, just to see what it is. Over the years, we have come to love the volunteers, because often what we try to cultivate, by clearing out the beds, watering and weeding, carefully mulching, are poor producers.

By contrast, nearly every volunteer plant that has ever grown in our garden has been prolific. A favorite story involves a surprise Hubbard squash crop we grew one year, and while we take credit for "growing" the squash, the only credit we deserve is the decision to buy the squash in the first place, because it looked cool, and we wanted to try it.

It was late fall, and the farmer's market was in its last days before closing for the season. There was still plenty to choose from, but most were things like squash that we only had a passing acquaintance with. We knew pumpkins, but most of the other Cucurbitaceae relatives were foreign to us. This particular squash was blue and kind of cool looking, which had been what captured our attention. It was shaped like a gourd, with a bulbous end tapering to a sort of handle. The outside was all bumpy and hard, like a shell. We bought one, out of pure curiosity.

And that one squash sat in our cold storage (the floor of our bedroom) for five months. In March or so, it became a case of use-it-or-lose-it, and we figured if we were going to try it, now would be better than later. We had no idea what we would find when we chopped it open.

Anyone who has ever tried Hubbard squash knows what happened when the gourd was placed on the counter and a knife for cutting into the flesh was selected. After a couple of minutes of trying to halve the squash, and much accompanying grunting and panting, a bigger, sharper knife was chosen. A few minutes later, the thing was finally cut into two pieces, and inside looked exactly like the inside of a pumpkin.

We cleaned out the seeds, and armed with a recipe from our favorite cookbook — the Internet — we hacked the squash into slices (no wimp's task, let me tell you), the pieces were placed in a baking dish, topped with chopped walnuts and drizzled with maple syrup. After baking for about a half hour, it was delicious, and even members of the family who refuse different foods on principle enjoyed it.

The seeds and cooked leftover hulls went into the compost pile, which had been moved for the winter to the middle of a garden bed. At the beginning of the season, we turn last year's summer pile and put the compost into the beds, and then the winter compost bin is moved into the summer bin. Most of the volunteers come from seeds that ended up in one of our two beds and did not fully compost.

Such was the case with the Hubbard squash volunteers. At first, I knew it was from the squash family, but unclear on what type, and by the time the fruit set, the twelve-foot vines were growing all over the back yard, over the fence, across the wood pile and into the driveway. It was such an impressive vine, that a carload of lost tourists, who had accidentally turned down our road, stopped to admire it and take pictures.

Having forgotten about the Hubbard squash, when fruit first appeared, we had no idea what it was, and so posted a picture to the blog. A reader correctly identified it as Hubbard squash. By the end of the summer, we had 180 pounds of the blue-skinned squash — our single biggest harvest ... ever.

This has become a favorite story to share, because it illustrates a couple of really awesome lessons. First, it is possible to grow quite a lot of food on a very small suburban lot. We had 180 pounds of Hubbard squash, which we calculated would last our family a month and a half, if we ate five pounds of squash per day. We might get sick of squash, but we would not starve.

The second important lesson is that plant foods grow — often in spite of our best efforts. In fact, the part B of this lesson is that food grows, and we just need to know where to find it. What is kind of funny, in an interesting not humorous way, is that try as we might, we have yet to plant Hubbard squash seeds that produce as well as those volunteer vines did — even when the seeds are planted in the same spot the volunteers seemed to enjoy so much.

As foragers, we discovered that we needed to pay close attention to what grows where. This knowledge is particularly important to us, because we know and are comfortable with such a finite number of plants. Knowing where to find them, and in what environment, is pretty crucial, if we hope to eat them.

As with gardening, there are plants that enjoy each other's company, happily growing side by side, helping the other grow healthy and strong. When done by gardeners with conscious intent, this is called companion planting. Nature seems to have a similar understanding of the way things should work. By making note of plants that coexist, it is possible to reasonably predict which plants will grow in a specific location based on those that are currently there.

This type of thinking is regularly used by mushroom hunters. When it comes to finding a particular mushroom, they commonly describe locations to search based on specific trees or terrains. For instance, during a mushroom walk this summer, we were advised to look under pine trees, in the typical litter on the forest floor, to find chanterelles. Similarly, we were advised to search birch trees for chaga.

As new as we are to foraging, we are even less educated in this line of thinking and knowledge. It may take years of observation to reliably draw these types of conclusions for other species of plants. We have yet to find a wild edibles guide that speaks specifically to this point, but we have started making mental notes. For instance, we know of a blueberry patch that we have visited for years. This year, for the first time, we noticed an abundance of wintergreen growing beneath the bushes. We also observed that sheep laurel (*Kalmia angustifolia*), which is not edible, grows in the same spot. While not completely understanding the significance of this observation, or how it might help us, we have noted similar patches of blueberry, sheep laurel and wintergreen growing elsewhere.

Several years ago, we were very fortunate to have a teacher from a local primitive skills school work with a group of home-schoolers at our house. We thought we knew a lot about what grew where in our neighborhood and that we would be able to help our teacher find the plants he wanted to teach us to use. We had, after all, lived in this neighborhood for a decade, and we believed we knew our way around pretty well. We found that we did not know as much as we thought.

On one hike across an area that had been formerly wooded, but had been razed for future development, he showed us our amazing patch of nettles. We had no idea it was there. We made a mental note: nettles like disturbed areas. On another, he wanted to show us how to harvest and use cattails. We thought we knew where we could find some, and we did, but the stand was in a drainage ditch, and the roots were not really fit for consumption. Cattails grow in marshy areas, which are sometimes polluted by residential run-off. It was a good lesson for us.

On a different day, walking in an area that was not quite as familiar, we pointed to a bush, and said, "Look! Hazelnut!" He asked how we could be sure it was hazelnut and not witch hazel (*Hamamelis*), and at that moment, not being familiar with witch hazel, we had never considered it was anything but hazelnut. The identification as hazelnut was correct, and back at the house, we showed our teacher why we knew it was hazelnut, when we introduced him to the volunteer hazelnut that had been growing for a few years underneath our oil tank. It had finally really started to thrive once we stopped using a gas-powered mower and running it over all summer long.

In expanding our own foraging areas, we began to notice patterns. Hazelnuts like to grow in dappled shade as woody underbrush but will produce more nuts if they have a few hours of sun, but they do not thrive in full sun (which is why the hazelnut likes growing under our oil tank. It is on the eastern side of the house and, by midafternoon, in the shade. Cattails seem to grow well with their roots wholly submerged in fresh water but also thrive on the periphery of the salt marsh, where their roots will be inundated only part of the day. Nettles will take root in a very sunny location in poor and/or disturbed soil. Blueberries like acidic soil, we are told, and they do seem to proliferate in pine forests, such as are common in our area.

Sometimes we made assumptions about what grows in an area, only to discover that the area was not exactly what we had expected. Dandelion, for instance, grows really well in fields, but not in fields of tall grass. It is a low-growing herb that likes to hug the ground and spread out. In our heavily mulched garden bed where it is not competing with any neighboring plants, the leaves grow a foot long and three to four inches wide. In the field that is mowed regularly, but where they compete with the grass for sun and nutrients, the plants are smaller. In the early spring, we might drive by a field and see hundreds of bright yellow dandelion flowers waving at us, but as the grass grows taller through the season, turning brown in the heat of the mid-summer days, the dandelions would be buried in the thigh-high stalks. When we went to fields where we found milk-weed, we did not find any dandelion.

Because we had a finite amount of time for foraging and a very limited number of plants that we could positively identify and use, knowing what we might find and where became very important. If we were setting out with the express purpose of foraging, we could not waste time by not finding what we sought.

One day, we decided to head out on a foraging trip. Our plan was to walk a mile or so up the road to the waterfall. Over the more than a decade we have lived in the area, we made it a point to visit the falls a couple of times each year. It is a really nice walk, and the falls were a quiet and beautifully natural place to hang out. Plus, we have found a couple of geocaches there. On our previous visits, back before really starting any foraging and just learning plant identification, we found berries on the path leading down to the stream, and we knew there was sweet fern. The goal on this particular mid-spring day was fiddleheads (*Matteuccia struthiopteris*). It was, we thought, the right time of year.

The falls were part of a larger property that was once a thriving hotel and family restaurant and some summer cabins. In its heyday, the waterfall and surrounding trails were part of the tourist draw for the summer rentals, and we were told that there was once a trail that meandered back to a pond somewhere back in the woods. We have never found the pond. Over time, the trail system fell to disrepair, just as the old hotel moldered and the cabins sat empty, even during the summer tourist season.

A few years ago, the whole acreage was purchased by a developer, who had a grand vision of a combined business park and housing development. The old hotel was razed along with the iconic yellow-roofed cabins. A couple of retail buildings have been erected on the property. A road with utilities for all of the future businesses was constructed back through the woods, and the trail system was re-vamped, including the addition of a parking area.

During the construction phase, we had avoided the area, but we remembered well the old trails with the narrow paths next to a twenty-foot drop-off and the uneven paths pockmarked with washed out rivulets, where each spring, melting snow and torrential rains robbed the path of a bit of soil. On our first visit since the development, we had no idea what to expect.

Taking our old path in, we found some modifications. Since the new trail system was maintained and a lot more level than the old one had been, the location was no longer a quiet, secluded spot, which made foraging a bit more of a challenge. There were people all over the place.

The other challenge was that, as much as we thought we knew the area, very few of the plants we came across were familiar. We found fiddleheads, but we were a couple of weeks too late for picking and eating. They were small and mealy-looking anyway. We also saw a broad-leafed plant that resembled a leaf lettuce, growing on the side of the little stream that meandered through the valley. It was not in our foraging book, and we did not know what it was, but we were sure it was edible. We took a leaf so that we could research the plant back home (we identified it as a plant commonly known as false hellebore [*Veratum virida*], which is not edible). Another spring green, Clintonia, most of which, like the fiddleheads, was just beyond the point of providing enough for a good meal, but the nibble we did take was very tasty.

While we did not end up with anything we could eat, the trip was not a total loss, because we learned a couple of really valuable lessons. The best lesson was about paying attention to the landscape and not making assumptions. We knew it was a heavily wooded, very wet area. What we were not prepared for was how unfamiliar the entire landscape would be to us.

We also learned that just because an area looks, at first glance, the same as another area, even one just a few miles away, does not mean the same sorts of plants grow there, because very subtle nuances can make the plants that thrive in the area very different. For example, we had never before seen the false hellebore we found growing on the sunny banks of the stream. We have a brook near our house, but had never seen those plants. The difference is that the stream at the falls gets more sun, largely due to annual flooding. The stream closer to our house is well contained in its banks, which it rarely breeches, and so the trees grow right up close, digging the roots deep, and there is not a lot of space for herbs to grow there.

The best way to forage is to simply get outside, slow down and walk around, listening and looking. This is really the only way to get to know an area, but when driving anywhere, we will pay attention to the plants growing along the road. We have found a lot of edibles with our high-speed foraging, and when we see a particularly desirable something, we will stop and pick it.

One day in the fall, we were sorely in need of a cold tonic, that is, white pine tea. White pine grows all through the woods behind our house, but there was no time, even for a short walk. Instead, we kept an eye out while traveling down the road on our way back from dropping the girls at their dance classes. We spied two small trees at the roadside, pulled over and harvested enough for a pot of tea. When driving from one place to another — to the library or to the girls' dance lessons — we pay attention to what is growing at the roadside, and sometimes, like with apples or white pine, our practice pays off in a big way.

Where we live is not better or worse for foraging than other parts of the world, just like it is not significantly better or worse for gardening. While we do have a shorter, colder growing season than elsewhere, some plants thrive here that just do not do as well in other places, and vice-versa.

When foraging, as with gardening, it is important to know what is available where one lives. Otherwise, foraging will be an incredibly frustrating activity.

CHAPTER 14

Persistence and Repetition Are Key

Knowing trees, I understand the meaning of patience.
Knowing grass, I can appreciate persistence.
—Hal Borland

HAVING GONE THROUGH MANY SEASONS OF FORAGING, especially this past year, where we incorporated it more as a way of life than simply a novel pastime, we can appreciate Hal Borland's quote all the more. Basing a portion of one's diet on what grows wild within a ten-mile radius of home can be quite a gamble, especially with limited time and knowledge.

We learned both patience and persistence over this project. The patience came in going more slowly, which sounds contradictory, especially after talking so much about our high-speed foraging adventures. Most of our foraging efforts were very thoughtful ventures, where we went to a specific place — often with the express purpose of looking for a specific food.

What is lucky for us was that sometimes, when we were searching for one thing, we would find another, which is how we found one of the most prolific blackberry brambles we harvested this year.

Southern Maine is home to the largest salt water marsh in the state. It was known to the Sokokis Indians, who lived in the area before the Europeans settled here, as *Owascoag*, which means "land of much grass." Luckily for us (and it), the community where this marsh is located has taken a very progressive stance with regard to land conservation. It has several land trust areas, including this beautiful little park on the tidal river that has been designated a protected area.

What is extra neat about the area is that someone has taken the time to not just set this piece of land aside, but they have also gone through and placed markers that show visitors where certain plants are growing, and often times how that particular plant is beneficial or not (like poison ivy). The park is home to several different habitats. At the entrance to the park is what was probably former pasture land that became a golf course and is now a field of tall grasses and milkweed. Walking down the mowed paths across the field, one enters a pine forest that includes a couple of frog ponds (where we also saw our first ever leech). Keep walking through the forest paths, and ultimately, one will come out into the wide vista that is the salt marsh. It is a pretty incredible journey filled with so much to see and experience.

We have spent a lot of time in the park. The first time we visited, it was in search of a geocache, which we found, but even better than finding the little treasure was discovering the sanctuary. We have returned many times since, both just for our own pleasure and also with our nature skills class. Most recently, our goal in visiting the sanctuary was to find wild edibles.

We knew there were apples there, but we were not quite prepared to discover berries (galore!), milkweed, cattail and white pine. We looked for mushrooms, but did not find them there, yet. There are dozens of grasses, covered with snails (and ticks), and over at the tidal river are the clam flats, where we had our bare-handed, clam-digging adventure.

What would be nice, for on-demand people like us, would be if we could take a Saturday, instead of our weekly trip to the local grocery store, head over to the river sanctuary and just gather what we want for the week, and everything we needed would be ready on our arrival, but that is not how it works. In the real world, apples and cattails do not ripen at the same time. In fact, sometimes green apples and red apples do not ripen at the same time. Sometimes a single stand of blackberry brambles will have berries at all stages from green to black and every color in between. Even the blackberries growing in the same location on the same bramble will not ripen at the same rate.

It was an important lesson for us. Like most average Americans, we have become accustomed to getting food at the grocery store, where everything is always ready to be eaten, right then (or after it is cooked). Even at the farmer's market or farm stand, the food will be ready to eat, and we do not need to know what an unripe blackberry looks like, because the folks there will not try to sell us unripe fruit. Buying food means that we do not need to know the stages of development for the plant foods with which we are most familiar.

Observing the different rates at which things ripened led us to understand Hal Borland's lesson about patience and perseverance. We learned that we have to watch and wait while the plant goes through its growing cycle, and when it is ready, we can take our third, but that is the other part of the lesson: there is no harvesting of a years' worth of wild foods in one visit. Many wild plants will not have a years' worth ready for harvest all at the same time, and if one observes the Forager's Rule of Thirds, then harvesting enough wild food to put some back requires many visits. With the blackberries, it took us three visits to get enough berries to enjoy on the spot and to have some to save for the winter.

When we go foraging, it is usually with the goal of finding some for now and having a bit left over so that we can put some in the freezer. It is very different from the way we approach PYO farms. We typically visit a PYO orchard or field with the purpose of picking enough to store most our harvest for the winter. For instance, we will pick forty-eight quarts of strawberries — most of which go to make our annual batch of strawberry jam. Depending on how hungry the girls are for strawberries and whether or not we meet our goal of two dozen pint jars of jam, we may need to go back, but we often only need to make one trip.

Apple picking is similar for us. We pick a couple of bushels for eating and canning. Sometimes we buy utility apples in bulk for canning, but we try to minimize our energy expenditure (the closest PYO strawberry field is thirteen miles from us, and the closest PYO apple orchard is thirteen miles in the other direction) by getting as much as we can the first time and not having to go back.

Wild apples grow all around us, are free to pick and, in most cases, are on our way to somewhere else, which means no special out-of-the-way trip to the PYO orchard. The only disadvantage is that we have to pay very close attention to when the apples are getting ripe so that we do not miss them, and then, we have to be willing to take a couple of extra minutes en route to give ourselves time to stop and pick.

In addition to returning to the same spot to harvest over the entire time that things ripen, we also learned to keep looking for plants that we wanted to pick. We had found many blackberry brambles early in the season, well in advance of the flowers growing, blooming and setting fruit. The plants that we found early did indeed produce fruit, but the berries were much smaller and less flavorful than those in the larger, more prolific spot that we found late in the season. Had we stopped looking at different plants, and for other locations for what we sought, we might not have been fortunate enough to find this abundant crop.

Seeking out specific plants can in itself be an arduous process, because they do not always grow in large clusters or colonies. After years of trying to grow hazelnuts, we found one growing under our oil tank. That began a search for other bushes in the area, which we did find. We stopped there, but during this project, we searched more, identifying nearly one dozen mature, nut-producing bushes within one hundred paces of our front door. Given the competition with the squirrels and chipmunks over harvesting, we will continue this search to ensure that we might harvest some for ourselves.

When it comes to foraging, there is no greater lesson than perseverance, and as people who grew up in an age in which everything we want is available on demand, this has probably been our most difficult lesson to master. It was a bit disappointing to set out to pick a particular plant, only to find out that it was not ready for harvest, was not growing where we expected, was over ripe by the time we got around to looking for it or had been eaten by animals or insects before we had a chance to take our third.

Avoiding any of those four disappointments requires us to spend a lot of time looking for food plants, going back again, and again, usually to the same place. This repetition gives us a feel for the area that a quick visit or that visits during only the spring or fall does not. Returning several times throughout the year allows us to become familiar with those local plants and how they mature.

Several times over the seasons, we set out to forage one thing and ended up with something else. During the fall, we hoped to gather some foods for a stew, did not find everything we wanted, but did bring home other plants, including burdock root. This was one we had hoped for but thought we had missed the opportunity to harvest.

Although we did not subsist for the year just on foraged food, we incorporated it into at least one meal a week. In fact, even into the winter, at the time of the writing of this book, we are still eating foods foraged over the growing seasons and continue to forage what is available. In particular, we harvest white pine, because it is one of the best teas for combating winter illnesses, like colds and the flu.

In foraging, failure is not the inability to find what one seeks, but rather not giving the task the attention it is due.

Part IV

How to Get Started

CREDIT: CRYSTAL ARSENAULT, CAPTURE THE
MOMENT PHOTOGRAPHY

Our guests were a little hesitant to try the milkweed lasagna, but, as the good sports that they are, gave it a taste.

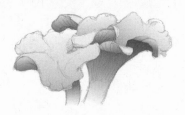

CHAPTER 15

Beginning Foraging

*I*F YOU HAVE FOOD ALLERGIES, OR VERY PICKY CHILDREN, *you may want to bring at least one dish you know you can eat. Most of the food will be locally grown, mostly in our yard, and probably some of it foraged:).* So read the invitation to the Second Annual Brown Family Summer Party. When we decided to work harder to bring foraged foods into our diet, a secondary goal was to share the bounty of our harvests with friends at our annual summer party.

Our friends have come to accept and expect odd things from us. Bringing the chickens home probably raised a few eyebrows; and the realization that we actually do not have a clothes dryer — by choice — will occasionally give some new acquaintances pause. Learning that we do not have a television, not just no cable, confused one new friend so badly that she offered to fundraise so that we could buy one. After those initial shocks, though, most learn to accept that sometimes we do things a little different from the norm. While putting a hole in the lid of a Mason jar and inserting a straw for my very own reusable to-go cup for taking my homemade sweet tea on the road (one just can't find the exact flavor of brewed sweet tea at any local shop) did not cause any stir, eating homemade soup at work out of a Mason jar (why bring it in a jar to transfer into a bowl?) did result in a few sideway glances at first. We have developed quite a reputation when it comes to food choices as well. One time we had invited some friends over for a group applesauce canning session, and our friend's daughter told her that she only liked "organic" canned foods, to which the friend replied, "Um, remember where I'm going."

Still, we were pretty sure that our intent to serve foraged foods at our party would cause a ripple of discontent, or at very least a flurry of regrets in answer to our invitation. Neither happened, and what did both surprised and delighted us.

"I foraged blueberries," a friend, who lives on a lake, informed us. She told us the story of how she got up one morning, hopped into her canoe, paddled across the lake to where she knew blueberries grew and picked enough to make the cake she brought to our party.

"I have as much goldenrod as anyone could want; plenty of grass and thistles and some of what I think are cattails. Plus poison ivy and some sumac, the kind with red flowers or whatever those things are. Any of that useful?" another friend asked. We declined the poison ivy, but after asking for more clarification on what he called sumac, we thought he probably had staghorn sumac. We were really excited because that is the key ingredient for survival lemonade. It was one of those things we had long wanted to try, but had just never got around to harvesting. Much to our delight, and surprise, he brought enough flowers for several pitchers of lemonade, which we shared among our guests.

While we made very clear our plan to harvest and serve local foraged foods, we never set any requirement that our guests follow suit. For previous parties, we had challenged invitees to bring local foods, but since foraging is still so new to even us, we had no intention of requiring that any gift of food meet some rigid standard.

The fact that any of our guests brought foraged food at all was incredibly exciting, and very humbling. It also reminded us that, while most people will automatically assume that they know nothing about foraging, insisting that they cannot identify any wild foods, the reverse is often true. Almost everyone we know can identify at least a handful of wild foods. Further, not only can they identify them, but they often harvest those foods *in lieu of purchasing them.*

They can identify these foods, many of which they even use regularly, but have a real disconnect in realizing that, even if the only thing they pick each year is a few berries, if they are harvesting wild foods, they are foragers. There seems to be some mistaken idea that to be a forager requires some in-depth knowledge of plants, even the weird ones like Clintonia or chanterelles that only a few professional foragers know. I agree, if people are going to teach foraging and guide foraging walks in the woods, they should know a bit more than just a few berries, but by regularly picking and eating foods that are not cultivated, one can honestly claim the title of forager.

For many years, we have been studying medicinal and edible plants, but it was only just over this past year that we finally gave ourselves permission to call ourselves foragers. We had taken classes and learned a few plants here and there, studied books and YouTube videos and discovered wild plants in the woods. Although we could identify dozens and knew which were edible, it was not until happening upon Connie and Arnold Krochmal's *A Naturalist's Guide to Cooking with Wild Plants* that we overcame our fear of wild foods and found a simple (and delicious) way to take the plants from the wilds to our plates.

This book helped us realize that wild plants need not be seen as exotic ingredients in some weird dish that only those raised with a particular palate can comfortably swallow. It also showed us that their preparation requires only very basic culinary skills and that many very tasty dishes can be made combining wild foods and some common ingredients: flour, eggs, oil, salt and pepper. Until we discovered this book, our experience with harvesting, preparing and eating wild foods was pretty limited, because we never practiced any of the knowledge that we had gained about plant lore.

Over the past decade, we have spent a lot of time getting to know our local area. We like to take leisurely strolls through the paths in the woods with our children and dogs, and when we stroll, we pay attention to what we see growing. Once we decided to really make foraging a part of our life rather than just some summer-day hobby, like picking trail nibbles when on a hike, we became keenly aware of how little we really knew. We realized that there will always be more to learn about local plants and we will never know everything, even about the plants we already forage. Some things that we have done right, however, can help others who might be interested in starting to forage.

I. There is no such thing as too many books.

For a very long time, we have been collecting foraging books. We love foraging books for good reason, and it all goes back to the goal of attaining self-sufficiency. There is nothing quite so freeing as being unafraid of hunger, of knowing that there is food growing out there, and most of it is free for the taking. There is nothing quite so empowering as knowing that, even if one does not have a paycheck, one can still eat.

A book devoted to foraging will have three basic pieces of information that are invaluable to a forager: how to identify the plant, how and when to harvest the plant and how to use the plant as food. These books are valuable, but because most of the authors are expert foragers, the vast amount of information can sometimes be overwhelming.

When it comes to foraging, one cannot be too careful. While there are not nearly as many poisonous plants as we might believe, there are a few. It is wise advice to err on the side of caution: if one is not 100 percent sure, do not eat it, which is why we also like to consult other books. When we discover a new plant, or decide we would like to try to find one listed in the foraging book, we reach for a book that is not devoted to wild edibles.

Our favorite plant identification book, *Weeds of the Northern US and Canada* by France Royer and Richard Dickinson, includes a key organized by flower color and a seedling guide. It is broken down by plant family type (aster family, milkweed family, etc.), with an explanation of each member (dandelion and burdock are both in the aster family). The book covers the plant habitat and habits, and (our favorite part) why one probably wants to eradicate the plant, i.e., why it is considered a weed. The back cover has a quote by Ralph Waldo Emerson, who is attributed with having observed, "What is a weed? A plant whose Virtues have not yet been discovered." We are learning to discover the virtue of common weeds.

Another favorite book, written by Thomas Elpel, is *Botany in a Day: The Patterns Method of Plant Identification*. In spite of the title, it contains far more information than can be digested in a single day. The benefit to learning the patterns of plant families quickly becomes evident. For instance, the first family, the mustard family, represents over 3,200 species of plants worldwide, all edible. By simply learning to recognize this family in the wild, one can now identify 3,200 species of plants that can be eaten. That is not bad for a single day's work. It follows that most of the plants within a family have similar properties, whether they are edible, medicinal or otherwise. Although we have yet to fully digest the entire book, we keep picking away at its secrets.

Between our seven or eight books devoted to wild edibles, the weed book that is invaluable for identifying the plants we find and *Botany in a Day*, we are comfortable that we are accurately identifying what we intend to eat. It cannot be stressed enough: do not eat a plant unless 100 percent sure of its identity.

II. Always check three sources when trying to identify a plant.

With all our books on wild edibles, medicinal plants and so-called weeds and trees, we probably could find three very different resources to help us verify the identity of a plant we have found, but we also like to cross-reference these discoveries using the Internet. We use online sources to find a name for the plant we are trying to identify, and then we can consult one of our print resources.

We research very carefully to be certain about what we have before we eat it. The other benefit to consulting several references is that different wild edibles books will give us varying ways to use the plant, resulting in a broader range of culinary possibilities. In addition, each author will have different experiences with the plant, and so we can determine if it is worth the time and effort that would be involved to harvest it and use it.

For instance, cattail has long been on our to-try list, and, indeed, we have attempted to harvest it on a couple of occasions. It is often referred to as "nature's grocery store" because so much of the plant can be used. After reading an article by renowned forager Wildman Steve Brill, we had to rethink whether we wanted to work really hard to get cattail root to be used as flour … or whether it might be better to just use the abundance of Jerusalem artichoke roots we already had easy access to. For us, having a wide variety of experiences to learn from is priceless.

Sometimes, though, we found ourselves getting stuck with our foraging. We would spend a great deal of time reading about a plant, learning to identify it and even going so far as finding it in the woods, but we needed that extra something to help get us to a point where we were comfortable that we really did know what we thought we knew.

III. Finding a teacher or a mentor can come in very handy.

Over the years, we have been incredibly fortunate to have many foraging teachers. The first plant walk we ever went on was through the educational center at the salt marsh. While the walk was not terribly successful for teaching us much, it did whet our appetite and send us looking for more.

In this particular instance, the walk included twenty adults with a plant expert guide, who led us through the marsh on several meandering trails. In the two hours with this expert, he pointed out more than fifty plants. Unfortunately, sometimes it was just a pointing-in-passing scenario, and so those of us in the back of the group often did not hear what was being said or what plant had just been identified. There were too many people, and the walk covered too many plants. We did come away with one very useful piece of information, however. The trunk of the poplar tree has a film that can be rubbed off with one's hands and was used as a sunscreen and insect repellant by natives in the area where we live.

We have been fortunate to find several other teachers and participate in many more walks over the years. One was guided by a member of a local native tribe. Unlike our first medicinal plant walk, this time our teacher (Freda Paul, a native Passamaquoddy) introduced us to only a few plants, among them, the white pine. He was very careful to show us the whole plant, to have us pay careful attention to the bark of the tree and the spread of the limbs. He taught us how to distinguish it from the many other members of the pine tree family, and the lesson we learned is that only the white pine has five fingers — that is, each tassel is made up of five leaves.

As we became more knowledgeable, we seemed to find teachers who did not just walk through a field, point to a plant and give it a name, but rather were very careful to ensure that we were really learning to see the plants as distinct and individual. So, like our lesson with the white pine, we would be shown a plant, like trout lily (*Erythronium americanum*), but more than just saying "This is trout lily," our teacher, Chris Knapp, (founder and co-owner of the Koviashuvik Local Living School in Temple, Maine) brought us down to the level of the plant. We really got to know the plant by observing its habitat (is it dry or wet, forested or field?), noting the texture, color and scent of the leaves, looking for any flowers, studying at the stems and paying attention to the root. Chris never pointed to a plant and declared, "That is [insert plant name]." Rather, when he wanted us to learn a plant, he introduced us, like a friend introducing a friend. Then, after we got to know the plant, we were taught how to use it to nourish our bodies. It was a whole learning experience from meeting the plant in the wild, to bringing it back to our campsite and making it into food.

Every teacher we have had since Chris has had a similar approach. Mike DiMauro, who works with the Maine Primitive Skills School, used the same method when teaching us about sarsaparilla (*Aralia nudicaulis*). It was never just pointing to the plant and naming it. We were encouraged to touch and smell and study the plant.

Of all of the plant types we have learned to identify, the most daunting has probably been mushrooms. We are far from being comfortable with mushrooms. There have only been a very few (like, two types) of the dozens and dozens growing wild that we were positive we could identify. For us, finding a mushroom expert was absolutely imperative, because mushrooms are highly beneficial as a foraged food, both for the nutritional value and for the caloric value.

We were incredibly fortunate to have Dan Agro leading us through the woods on a gourmet mushroom walk. What was also remarkable about Dan was that he never pretended to know what he did not know. From the beginning, he was very straightforward with us in explaining that his expertise was with gourmet edible mushrooms, and that was what he showed us. Like our other teachers, he did not just point and declare "There is the mushroom you seek." He also taught us to use all of our senses when finding and identifying mushrooms. He advised us to look closely and ask ourselves questions, like what does the part that comes out of the ground look like? Does it have gills? What color is it? He also encouraged us to touch it and sniff it, carefully, of course.

On that warm, drizzly late summer day, as we plodded through the pine-needle strewn undergrowth and waded across washouts and tripped over fallen limbs, Dan educated us on the symbiotic relationship between the huge pines and the tiny mushrooms. We learned interesting little factoids: some mushrooms do not actually grow in the dark, but need a bit of dappled sunlight. When a member of our group was fortunate enough to spot the tiny stand of the elusive chanterelle, we learned that they smell like apricots, and a mycelium expert can smell mushrooms in the air.

There is so much information to learn, and going on plant walks can be an incredibly overwhelming experience, as we learned on our first foray. Our mistake that first walk was not taking full advantage of the opportunity to learn from our teacher, but we have never made that mistake again, and now, even if we don't ask questions, we always remember to take notes.

IV. Take lots of notes.

Of course, that advice extends beyond the expert walks and into our own forays into the suburban wilds around our home. Keeping a journal of the plants we find, including making some drawings, or snipping a bit of the plant to press into the pages has helped us on a few occasions to identify plants. An additional benefit to a journal is that we can refer to it later in the season or in subsequent years. Writing down what we see when we are out, or even just where we went on a particular day, can be valuable information later.

Sometimes our journal is not writing on a page but pictures of a particular area. In fact, during this year-long foraging project, one of our favorite series of photos is of the field near our house taken over a six-week period, showing the progression from mid-spring to the beginning of the summer. Looking back at those was a startling reminder of how fast the season progresses and that we cannot waste time, because the season will not wait for us to be ready.

The journal can also be a very good tool, especially the pictures, for showing us what a particular plant might look like through its life cycle, which is very important to know because some plants are edible as young shoots but if eaten later will make one very sick. Pokeweed, a very popular spring green in the southern US, is quite tasty when it is picked young. However, later in the season, after the plant starts to flower, it can be toxic. Getting to know the plant through its entire progression from spring shoot to fall seed gives a whole picture.

V. Learn one or two plants in a season.

With so many plants to know, and so many that start out looking like others, the best thing a novice forager can do is to learn one or two plants in a season. In the very early days of learning to forage, we wasted a lot of time. Like that first foraging walk, where the only thing we learned was sunscreen (and we cannot eat sunscreen), we spent too much time poring over volumes of foraging books and trying to memorize every plant that we might see in a given season. It was a little like trying to shoot a target with buckshot. We might hit the bull's-eye and find what we want and actually successfully use it, but the usual result was that we would study the foraging book, and then when actually in the field, we would find nothing that looked like the picture in the book.

We knew there was food out there, and we wanted all of it, now. We were very much a product of our on-demand culture where we learn to memorize a lot of facts and trivia in school, which we regurgitate for the test. Since we were both excellent students and good test takers, there is some (not unfounded) belief that simple memorization is the same as knowing. As foragers, we have discovered that having a piece of information in our brain does not mean that we know anything at all.

Finally, we stopped trying to know everything through some magic of osmosis, some ridiculous belief that we would magically have all of the information there was to have about plants by reading about them, and we started the real work of learning about those we hoped to eat.

We admitted our ignorance and limitations, we slowed down, and we concentrated our efforts on learning one or two plants in a season. The result was that when we went on the walk with Dan Agro, for instance, the goal was to learn to identify, without fail, one mushroom. One. And if we did not get anything else out of the experience, that would be okay, because we would be one mushroom wiser than we had been at the start of the class.

We found that, even though each of the teachers was fantastic, we still must recognize how we learn. Our teachers did a fantastic job presenting each plant, introducing us to our new friends, but we still had questions.

VI. Ask questions.

We each come with our own unique learning style and set of experiences. Through our individual frames of reference, information can range anywhere between crystal clear and simple to dark and murky. Even in the confines of our own homes, we can ask questions. They can lead to further research in books or online, but can also result, through careful consideration, in deep understanding.

Question the type of soil in which a plant grows, or the time of year it blossoms, or the types of insect it attracts. These inquiries have led us to the answers we sought, if we truly desired to follow where they lead.

VII. Keep a calendar, or historical time line, of the progress of the environment as a whole.

As spring wends its way to summer, summer to fall and back through winter, different plants will sprout, bloom and fruit at their own rates. Animals, and insects, will follow suit in concert with those plants they eat. Keeping a record of bird sightings, or flowers blooming or shoots breaking through the soil allows one to keep time with the rhythm of the natural world. Over time, one can develop an intuitive feel for this rhythm as it shifts from season to season. This understanding can help foragers of all levels prevent missed opportunities, like an early maple sugaring season. At very least, this pleasant occupation connects one with nature. At best, it is a powerful tool in the foraging bag-of-tricks.

VIII. Heed the Rule of Thirds.

The Rule of Thirds is one of the most important things to learn when beginning to forage, because it is so tempting to harvest everything.

If one falls victim to this urge, the hunt will need to begin anew the following year with the search for a new source. Following this rule, one encourages the plants, or animals, to grow stronger and healthier. It also leaves the forager with the knowledge of where a particular food may be found, and it leaves the environment healthy by encouraging biodiversity. One should not look out solely for one's own benefit, but for the benefit of all of the beings with whom we live.

The advantage of knowing very early on that we intended to serve foraged foods at our party was that we were always on the lookout for things to share. Still, the idea of foraging enough food for our fifty-some guests was a bit daunting. As it turned out, we need not have worried.

The table was heaped with exactly what one should expect in a potluck dinner. On one side, there was a Mexican-style three-bean dip and a bag of tortilla chips from one guest, a couscous casserole that the guest was delighted to share was all local except for the couscous, and a blueberry cake made with foraged blueberries from another guest. In the middle was a tribute to Mediterranean fare with the plate of kabobs as they came off the grill, stuffed grape leaves and baklava, all of which included mostly ingredients grown on our nanofarm. At the other end of the food table sat our foraged dishes, including blackberry cobbler and milkweed pod lasagna.

As the sun set and the party started to wind down, the bulging clouds, which had graciously held their water long enough for us to entertain our guests with good eats and great musical entertainment provided by our talented daughters, let loose their heavy load of precipitation. We hurried to clear off the tables as the big rain drops soaked us.

Good food, good drink and good company are the essential elements to any gathering of human beings. Celebrations are never celebrations without the addition of food, and food is an integral part of our human existence — not just because we need food to survive, but also because it is our way of sharing. From birth to death, and all events in between, when we gather together, we bring food.

There was nothing quite so amazing through our whole experience of feeding ourselves foraged food, at least one meal per week for a year, as being able to share this passion for found food with our friends, who, whether wisely or not, never expressed concern about our plans to feed them this wild stuff.

And it was that coming together of friends for a communal feast to celebrate our success as foragers that made every moment absolutely worthwhile.

Bibliography

Preface

1. Krochmal, Connie and Arnold. *A Naturalist's Guide to Cooking with Wild Plants*. Quadrangle, 1974.

Chapter 1

1. Elpel, Thomas. *Botany in a Day: The Patterns Method of Plant Identification, 5th Edition*. HOPS Press, 2010.

Chapter 3

1. Jerusalem artichokes, www.nutrition-and-you.com/jerusalem-artichoke.html
2. Buhner, Stephen Harrod. *Healing Lyme: Natural Healing and Prevention of Lyme Borreliosis and Its Coinfections*. Raven Press, 2005.
3. Royer, Francis and Richard Dickinson. *Weeds of the Northern US and Canada*. Lone Pine Publishing, 1999.
4. Thayer, Samuel. *The Forager's Harvest: A Guide to Identifying, Harvesting, and Preparing Edible Wild Plants*. Birchwood, 2006.

Chapter 5

1. Maine Forestry Department. *Forest Trees of Maine.*
2. Katz, Sandor. *Wild Fermentation: The Flavor, Nutrition, and Craft of Live-Culture Foods.* Chelsea Green Publishing, 2003.
3. Amount of alcohol in a beverage, www.alcoholcontents.com/
4. Buhner, Stephen Harrod. *Sacred and Herbal Healing Beers: The Secrets of Ancient Fermentation.* Brewers Publications, 1998.

Chapter 6

1. Hardy, Kerry. *Notes on a Lost Flute: A Field Guide to the Wabanaki.* Downeast, 2009.

Chapter 7

1. Spahr, David. *Edible and Medicinal Mushrooms of New England and Eastern Canada: A Photographic Guidebook to Finding and Using Key Species.* North Atlantic Books, 2009.

Chapter 8

1. www.sfgate.com/health/article/Stomach-flu-is-really-food-poisoning-3913858.php
2. usatoday30.usatoday.com/money/industries/food/2008-02-17-slaughterhouse-recall_N.htm
3. money.howstuffworks.com/10-food-recalls.htm
4. en.wikipedia.org/wiki/Genetically_modified_food
5. www.naturalnews.com/034812_GMO_corn_soy.html
6. FDA, "Statement of Policy: Foods Derived from New Plant Varieties" (GMO Policy), Federal Register, Vol. 57, No. 104, p. 229.
7. www.huffingtonpost.com/jeffrey-smith/genetically-modified-soy_b_544575.html
8. www.ienearth.org/docs/what-countries-have-banned-gmo-crops.html
9. www.medicalnewstoday.com/articles/120264.php

10. www.extension.umn.edu/distribution/horticulture/DG2543.
    html

11. www.naturalnews.com/028819_BPA_intestines.html

12. Mann, Charles. *1491: New Revelations of the Americas Before
    Columbus*, 2nd Edition. Vintage Books, 2011.

Chapter 9

1. Food Price Index chart, www.fao.org/worldfoodsituation/wfs-
   home/foodpricesindex/en/

2. Price of oranges, www.nodeju.com/17851/orange-prices-go-
   through-the-roof.html

3. NPR article, John Boyd quote, www.npr.org/2012/08/14/1587
   62418/is-drought-slowly-killing-us-farms

4. Food riots resulting from crop failures and scarcity, www.
   commondreams.org/view/2011/01/10-1

5. Jobless rate (real numbers), www.factcheck.org/2012/02/whats-
   the-real-jobless-rate/

6. Homeless rate increases, usatoday30.usatoday.com/news/nation/
   2009-07-09-homeless_N.htm

7. Number of food stamp recipients increase, www.businessweek.
   com/news/2012-01-25/gingrich-calling-obama-food-stamp-
   president-draws-critics.html

Index

About the Authors

WENDY BROWN AND ERIC BROWN are suburban homesteaders growing roots (both literally and figuratively) in Southern Maine. They have been studying wild edibles for many years. Wendy is also the author of *Surviving the Apocalypse in the Suburbs*.

CREDIT: CRYSTAL ARSENAULT, CAPTURE THE MOMENT PHOTOGRAPHY

If you have enjoyed *Browsing Nature's Aisles* you might also enjoy other

BOOKS TO BUILD A NEW SOCIETY

Our books provide positive solutions for people who want to
make a difference. We specialize in:

**Sustainable Living • Green Building • Peak Oil
Renewable Energy • Environment & Economy
Natural Building & Appropriate Technology
Progressive Leadership • Resistance and Community
Educational & Parenting Resources**

For a full list of NSP's titles, please call 1-800-567-6772 *or check out our website* at:

www.newsociety.com